Harmony With The Movement Of The Universe

A Collection of Writings on Aikido and Yoga

Wayne F. Tourda
Vincent D. McCullough

Saddleback College

The McGraw-Hill Companies, Inc.
Primis Custom Publishing

New York St. Louis San Francisco Auckland Bogotá
Caracas Lisbon London Madrid Mexico Milan Montreal
New Delhi Paris San Juan Singapore Sydney Tokyo Toronto

McGraw-Hill

A Division of The ***McGraw-Hill*** *Companies*

HARMONY WITH THE MOVEMENT OF THE UNIVERSE

A COLLECTION OF WRITINGS ON AIKIDO AND YOGA

McGraw-Hill's Primis Custom Publishing consists of products that are produced from camera-ready copy. Peer review, class testing, and accuracy are primarily the responsibility of the author(s).

1 2 3 4 5 6 7 8 9 0 BBC BBC 9 0 9 8

ISBN 0-07-228245-2

Editor: Julie Kehrwald
Cover Design: Cynthia Nielson
Printer/Binder: Braceland Brothers, Inc.

The Authors

Celebrate

the

Temporary

Dedication

To Our Teachers

ACKNOWLEDGMENTS

Behind this text are numerous helping hands whose support and inspiration made this publication possible. To all these people, we owe our gratitude.

We would like to express our deep appreciation to Dr.Virginia Meyn, who worked long and patiently in the production of this text. Dr. Meyn not only contributed her literary expertise, but oversaw the orchestration of the entire book. We cannot say often enough that this book would not have been possible without her.

Thanks to Professor Nancy Bessette for her generous contributions to the yoga section, for not only writing the chapters on the Asanas and Relaxation, but working with the team long hours into the night on the text as a whole, with special attention to the bibliography(!).

To Troyce Thome, who somehow managed to balance the rigors of parenthood, teaching and publishing, we are greatly in her debt: for the layout of the book as a whole, for managing the yoga section and contributing several essays, and for her blithe spirit.

We are grateful to Cynthia Neilson, a professional artist who generously volunteered her expertise in the design and creation of the magnificent cover and the entire graphics in the book. We cannot thank her enough for the gift of her time and talent.

Thanks very much to our student Raul Terrado, whose photographic skills seem to capture each photo at the right moment. Thanks also for his willingness to help in many other ways as well. And to our friend Davida Wendorf, for modeling for some of the Asanas.

To our student Rochelle Higgs, who volunteered considerable time and effort with the bibliography, typing, and overall layout, we offer deepest thanks. She was always there for us, and she was always an inspiration.

And to all those individuals who experienced and endured the many hardships associated with the production of this text, we are grateful: to the Thome family; to Michael Ward, Steve Curry, and Rose Solomon for assisting us in our classes; to Dean Terrill Robinson, Susan Garant, and Lorna Hixon, in the Division of Physical Education and Athletics, for their support; to the library staff at Saddleback College, in particular, Bonnie Stephenson, for her indefatigible research of the bibliography.

Finally, we want to thank Dr. Lori Parker, chief instructor of Mumonkan-Do Dojo in Irvine, California, and her assistant Sensei Doug McBratney, who have withstood the pressures of mediocrity in their search for the Way.

COMMENTS FROM PROJECT PARTICIPANTS

My goodness, what a lucky student I am to have been involved with this text. "Suit up and show up" and good things will happen – that's what They say. This experience has been so enjoyable, I'm sorry to see it end. The work has been interesting, but what's really made it fun is working with the masterminds of this project. I'm very fortunate to have had this time with them.

Rochelle Higgs

My experience as graphic illustrator and digital imager for this book has been a fulfilling one. Together with exemplary mentors, Professors McCullough and Tourda, along with the rest of the staff, we combined our many talents as well as our love for Aikido and Yoga to share our collective knowledge with the greater community.

In this hectic world of technology, yoga brings us into balance and focus. It cleanses the mind and rejuvenates the body. If I miss a day, I really feel it.

At an early age I was drawn to yoga by the stretch (I thought it was a different form of gymnastics!). Gradually I became aware of how vital the breath is in the practice of the Asanas. As I began teaching yoga, I saw what a difference it made in people's lives; I even witnessed changes in individuals after one class. One learns through yoga, perhaps more than any other discipline, how rewarding helping others and having a positive impact can be.

Cynthia Neilson

I love Aikido and Photography. They are two disciplines of different arts. One is an art of "doing" and the other is an art of "watching." I have never had the opportunity to combine these arts as a project until Tourda Sensei and Mr. McCullough decided to publish this book. Sensei gave me this once in a lifetime chance. I am honored to be part of a team that has worked hand-in-hand in the spirit of unity toward a common goal.

To Tourda Sensi and Mr. McCullough: Thank you very much for this opportunity!

Raul S. Terrado

EDITOR'S PREFACE

It is with great interest that I have watched Vince McCullough build the Eastern Studies Program within the Physical Education Department at Saddleback College. From the inception of the first Yoga classes during the late 1960's to the Karate and Kung Fu classes in the 1970's and finally to the Aikido program in 1984, thousands of students and faculty have had the opportunity to share cross-cultural experiences with our Pacific Rim trading partners. As a former faculty member at Saddleback College, I have also enjoyed taking part in the Program as a student. Vince and his colleague Wayne Tourda are first-class instructors; they both have a unique talent for grounding the mystical wisdom of the East in simple, practical techniques without which the great ancient teachings remain largely inaccessible to the Western mind. They are, moreover, first-class academicians. Both of them have advanced graduate degrees from prestigious universities in the United States in addition to rigorous on-site training by native masters in their disciplines.

It therefore gives me enormous pleasure and pride to be a part of such a fine Program in the creation of a textbook that, in its first edition, attempts to encapsulate the best of their work thus far and to present a collection of some of the finest readings and illustrations to be found in a professional publication. A special note to the serious student: The book should be appreciated in its entirety, not merely in sections. As the principle of mind/body connection provides the theme of the book, so Yoga and Aikido are meant to be viewed here both in theory and application as an interconnected whole or, better perhaps, as complementary parts of that whole. I urge you, then, whether you are a student of Aikido or of Yoga, to read the whole text! You will see the threads that link the parts . . . and, hopefully, you will find your own connection within.

Virginia MacIvor Meyn, Ph.D. Comparative Literature, Yale '66
Professor Emeritus, English and Humanities, Saddleback College

TABLE OF CONTENTS

LIST OF ILLUSTRATIONS

INTRODUCTION

Life is a struggle. We struggle to be born, we struggle in our daily interactions with other people, we struggle in school to make the grade, we struggle in the business world to make a living, we struggle with our beliefs, we struggle with our death. What makes the struggle worthwhile and brings us the inevitable joy that accompanies the breakthrough experience? Tenacity. Perseverance. How do we learn to stay the course? By finding a good mentor. But how do we find a mentor if we do not have the capacity to respect? There is a saying in the martial arts that "when the student is ready the teacher comes. Hence everything has its season." You cannot lead until you become a good follower. To respect takes humility, a willingness to lower oneself before one can rise. One cannot jump until one first bends one's knees, one has to come down before one can go up. O n e h a s t o b e e m p t y.

Pranayama or breathing control in Yoga teaches us how to empty ourselves; it teaches us how we must first breathe out before we breathe in, for example. In Aikido, the simple gesture of bowing before entering the dojo or practice hall demonstrates a sincere reverence and inspires an atmosphere conducive to the practice of Aikido, which is a symbolic re-enactment of life's struggle. In the techniques of Aikido and in the *asanas* or postures of Yoga, one learns that finding the center of that struggle is the key to right living. It is all about centering, about balance. The Bhagavad-Gita says that

For the uncontrolled there is
no wisdom.
For the uncontrolled
no concentration.
For the unconcentrated
no peace.
For the unpeaceful
no happiness can be.

Our text provides a collection of voices that teach ways of centering, its preparation and its practice. Since Aikido is said to share more characteristics in common with Yoga than with any of the other martial arts, we have chosen to pair these two nonviolent disciplines. Both aim to unite the practitioner with the universal and thus to create an atmosphere of harmony within and without.

It is hoped that this little text will offer support for those who are seeking the Way.

Professor Wayne F. Tourda (Doshin)
Professor Vincent D. McCullough (Buddhaprem)
June 1998, Mission Viejo, California

Aikido

WHY STUDY A MARTIAL ART?
By Herman Kauz

Most apparent and easily visible are the results of the physical exercise encountered in training. Pursuing a regimen of regular physical exercise helps promote better physical and mental health. We might find that we are seldom ill and that we have sufficient energy to do our day's work without becoming overly tired. Certainly, we become physically stronger and our body attains, or retains, a youthful look in which the muscles are firm and excess fat is absent. This exercise also serves as a harmless outlet for frustration and helps to relieve the damaging physical and mental effects of the stress of modern life.

Equally visible, but requiring a longer period of time to appear, is the learning of a skill. We become able to use our body effectively in defense. Our movements grow more efficient and we learn to conserve energy. Also, we become aware that we must subject ourselves to discipline if we are to practice diligently enough to attain the skill we seek. The external form of discipline characteristic of martial arts training gradually becomes internalized as we realize that in order to become accomplished in anything we must persevere in our practice over some years.

On another level, the growth of self-understanding and an increased knowledge of others are promoted by martial arts training. These capacities should develop in all of us as we grow older and gain experience in living. However, training of the sort encountered in martial arts is designed to enhance the growth of these qualities. Nevertheless, it is somewhat difficult to measure and assess the nature of this growth because it develops slowly and is, beyond question, affected by the lives we lead outside the training hall.

We also become aware of the value of employing a more intuitive way of relating to life than has been the custom in our society. Aspects of our training are designed to encourage the growth and use of this faculty by relaxing or giving reduced play to the logical, analytical portion of the mind. Logical reasoning and analysis is not negated but is given the appropriate and indispensable task of weighing, measuring, ordering and making coherent the world we are a part of. However, this capacity is not permitted to occupy the whole field to the extent that we ignore or are frightened or suspicious of information about ourselves or others that comes from other levels or areas of the mind.

Finally, we become able, with varying degrees of success, to focus our mind on each passing moment. We learn to act without thinking of where we have been or where we are going. Thoughts of past and future are usually irrelevant and will inhibit action. If our mind strays from complete attention to the matter at hand, our position grows weaker. Moreover, conscious or analytical thoughts at such times block or distort the freshness of the moment. We no longer really see what is happening, but are busy comparing and analyzing.

The gradual outcome of martial art training might be said to be the growth of maturity. The physical and mental settling that occurs gives us a calm approach to the exigencies of daily life, a bearing that is not easily upset. We are to a lesser extent than most caught up in the sometimes frantic pace characteristic of modern life. But where quick action is appropriate and necessary, we find ourselves adequate to the emergency. As we go as quietly as possible about our daily round, we find ourselves more awake in the sense of seeing ourselves and others with additional clarity. We become increasingly alert to what we are doing and what is going on around us. Conducting ourselves in this way stems from an inner strength or mental state which martial arts training has planted and helped nurture. Continued training provides the reinforcement necessary for the proper growth of this valuable plant.

THE PURPOSE OF MARTIAL ARTS TRAINING

Introduction to Eugen Herrigel's Zen in the Art of Archery (excerpt)
By D.T. Suzuki

One of the most significant features we notice in the practice of the martial arts as they are studied in Japan is they are not intended for utilitarian purposes only or for purely aesthetic enjoyments, but are a means to train the mind, indeed to bring it into contact with reality.

The mind first has to be attuned to the unconscious. If one really wishes to be master of an art, technical knowledge is not enough. One has to transcend technique so that the art becomes an "artless art" growing out of the unconscious. This state of unconsciousness is realized only when, completely empty and rid of the self, he becomes one with the perfecting of technical skill.

WHAT IS AIKIDO?

By Wayne Tourda

Aikido is first and foremost a martial art. It is perhaps one of the most effective means by which one can choose to defend oneself. However, the self-defense aspect is only a very small part or a by-product overemphasized by many practitioners as a result of a failure to comprehend Aikido in its entirety. Aikido is much more than a martial art. It is a medium or great vehicle enabling us as practitioners to unite with the infinite. When we are practicing Aikido, our mind is released from the many problems we have experienced throughout the day. Our mind is allowed to rest by not thinking.

Aikido was founded by Morihei Ueshiba, who after many years of struggle within himself realized that the true enemy is deep inside, and that we must look within for the answer, then win over ourselves. The amount of time we spend training is important, but what is more important is the transference of these values learned during practice, such as courtesy, respect, cooperation and benevolence, into our daily lives. It is true, conflict does exist in everyday life. However, it is our mission to transcend this discord and bring back into balance and complementarity those elements that are in opposition.

Aikido is not a sport. It is a process of education by which discipline is used to link mind, body, and spirit. It is a means of personal refinement and spiritual growth. Zen teaches us that

> the Master in the art of living makes little distinction between his work and his play, his labor and his leisure, his mind and his body, his education and his recreation, his love and his religion. He hardly knows which is which. He simply pursues his vision of excellence in whatever he does, leaving others to decide whether he is working or playing. To him he is always doing both.

WHY STUDY AIKIDO?
"The Art of Loving Combat"
By George Leonard

Aikido isn't for the person who is interested in getting a quick self-defense fix or acquiring an instrument for his anger and aggression. Though the students take turns playing the attacker's role, the art itself has no aggressive moves. It uses the attacker's energy and intention to confound him, and its ultimate aim is peace and harmony. Aikido is a lifelong journey with many sinuous twists and turns, many opportunities for patience and humility. Even world class athletes must be willing to endure periods of clumsiness, and the words "mastering aikido" constitute a self-canceling phrase. Analyzing the physics of Aikido in the July 1980 Scientific American, Jearl Walker concludes that "it is the most difficult of all the martial arts to learn. Its demands for skill, grace, and timing rival those of classical ballet."

All this being so, why should anyone dedicate himself to this art? It offers, first of all, superb all-around physical conditioning, involving the elements of strength, flexibility, coordination, balance, relaxation, and concentration. (The wind training in Aikido can be anaerobic or aerobic, depending upon the intensity and duration of practice sessions.) It contributes greatly to self-confidence. Just taking the falls demanded of the attacker's role – transforming the fear of falling into the joy of flying – makes you far more sure of yourself on life's sometimes uneven path. It provides the kind of regular, never-ending practice that is rare in our culture: something reliable to fall back on during nerve-racking times. And finally, after a few years training, it becomes a powerful and highly effective form of unarmed self-defense, perhaps the very best, since it aims ultimately at the end of all conflict. Even a student with only few weeks' training is likely to gain protection from an attack, though not through physical technique but rather through a change in attitude toward conflict and through the development of a more self-confident stance.

Fourteen years ago Aikido came to me as a totally unexpected gift. When a friend asked me to join him in a class, I had to confess I knew nothing about the martial arts and had never heard of Aikido. But I was soon captivated by the beauty and mystery of its physical movements, and reach and depth of its philosophy. After five years of training I passed my black-belt examination. A year later I was offered a chance to start an aikido school with two fellow aikidoists: Wendy Palmer, the radiant and gifted teacher described earlier in this article, and Richard Heckler, a psychologist, author, and former world-class sprinter. Over a period of eight years, several hundred students have passed through our school. Fourteen of those who have persevered now hold the yudansha rank.

As for the three of us, we keep right on training, thinking of ourselves less as teachers than as students, lifelong learners of an art that can never be mastered. Each of us teaches twice a week and trains as a student two or three times more. And if, on certain cold winter nights, we walk a little slowly and reluctantly up the dojo stairs, we are still rewarded: even the most ordinary night of Aikido is about as good as anything ever gets. And then, once in a very long while, there are the moments of sheer magic that occur in all intensely played physical arts, perhaps more frequently in Aikido than in some others. Some moments are likely to come when you least expect them: on a night when you're not feeling well, or maybe when you're near exhaustion from particularly strenuous training. Nevertheless, there you are in the calm center of the storm, with three attackers doing their very best to grab you, strike you, wrestle you down, and you have nothing at all to do except stay in the center and let yourself move with the attacker's moves, seeing without looking, hearing without listening, knowing without thinking. You are always here, it is always now, and there is only harmony, harmony.

Then it's over, and you come back slowly, breathing very hard, the lights seeming very bright. How long was it? Maybe twenty or thirty seconds. Not long, but long enough for a glimpse into how things might be, how, in essence, things perhaps are: an experience you can't keep but will always have.

AIKIDO AND THE MIND OF THE WEST

By George Leonard

Aikido is a Japanese art of self-defense. Those who have watched demonstrations of judo or jiu-jitsu may note certain similarities upon first visiting an aikido dojo (place of practice). There are the quilted gi uniforms, the colored belts, the resounding slaps of open palms on the mat, the Japanese terms (shomen-uchi irimi-nage!) that roll off the Western tongue with such esoteric yet innocent charm. But the differences – the characteristics that set aikido apart from the other martial arts – soon become apparent.

The defender takes his stand on the mat. He is relaxed yet alert. He offers none of the exotic defensive poses popularized by the movie and television action thrillers. An attacker rushes at him, but he remains calm until the last instant. There follows a split second of unexpected intimacy in which the two figures, attacker and attacked, seem to merge. The attacker is sucked into a whirlpool of motion, then flung through the air with little or no effort on the part of the defender, who ends the maneuver in the same relaxed posture, while the attacker takes a well-practiced roll on the mat. Unlike judo, aikido has no rules, no static opening positions; the throws are more fluid, the movements more like a dance. The nonaggressive nature of this art is reflected in its terminology. The defender is known as the nage (pronounced nah-gay), from a Japanese word meaning "throw." The attacker is called the uke (oo-kay), from a Japanese work associated with the idea of falling. Thus, in aikido, he who attacks takes a fall.

The art of aikido may achieve a transcendent beauty in the randori, or mass attack, when a single nage is set upon by four or more uke. Whirling, dancing, throwing, the nage seems to travel along unfamiliar lines of space-time. Seemingly trapped by converging attackers, he is, suddenly, not there. He moves easily in the midst of ferocious blows and flying tackles, not by opposing but by joining. He deals with the strongest attack by embracing it, drawing it into a circle of concord which, he feels, somehow joins him with the essential unity and harmony of the universe. He has no thought for his own safety or for any goal of external dominance. He is always here, it is always now, and there is only harmony, harmony. Such grace under pressure, it must be said, comes only after many years of practice and devotion. Mastery of aikido, as of any complete sport, stands entirely outside the familiar American doctrine of Ten Easy Lessons.

My own involvement with aikido began in November 1970. Never having heard of the art, I entered training with the utmost naivete, after an enthusiastic phone call from a friend. The call came at the right moment; I was just beginning an extended period of research and writing and was grateful for anything that might force me into a schedule of regular physical workouts. During the first few weeks I was often impatient with the hours spent on the nonphysical exercises—calming and centering my body, sensing the approach of others, blending with putative "energy flows," meditating.

My first teacher, Robert Nadeau, had studied several of the martial arts. At age sixteen, he had taught judo to policemen. He went on to spend four years as a police officer himself. Turning to the gentler, more spiritual art of aikido, he traveled to Japan to study for two and a half years in the dojo of Master Morihei Ueshiba, the founder of the art, who was then in his late seventies. I was amazed to hear Nadeau describe himself as "basically a meditation teacher." This man, with his great knowledge of self-defense, with his smooth, flawless physical techniques, a *meditation teacher*? Nadeau explained that competition is forbidden in aikido. Competition is limiting. Furthermore, it is not the way the universe operates. We would learn by cooperating, not competing, with each other. "Aikido's spirit," according to Master Ueshiba, "is that of loving attack and that of peaceful reconciliation."

My head could understand all this well enough. By that period of my life, however, I had learned to delight in competition and aggressive physical action. Some time was to pass before I began to incorporate Nadeau's teaching into my body and being. As it turned out, aikido has given me as much physical action as I could wish; and it obviously can be an effective mode of self-defense. But I have found – and this is the most important thing—that aikido's basic teachings erase those barriers the Western mind has erected between the physical and the mental, between action and contemplation.

Western thought, unlike that of the East, has by and large rejected direct experience as a path to the highest knowledge. Plato vacillates on this point but finally seems to conclude that experience can only remind us of what we already know. His approach to knowledge remains largely dialectical and cognitive. The Manichaean and Neoplatonic degradation of embodiment, eloquently expressed in Saint Augustine, widened the gap between sensory and "true" knowledge. The inflexible rationality of medieval thought left little room for subjective verification. In reaction, the scientific revolution of the sixteenth and seventeenth centuries became, as Alfred North Whitehead reminds us, "through and through an anti-intellectualist movement. It was the return to the contemplation of brute fact.""

But the "fact" of the scientific philosophers was not personal fact. Galileo, Kepler, Descartes, and Newton lived in a dream world of forces and motion and manipulation without touch or taste or color or smell. Later, Locke and Hume and the Positivists might have been expected to bring us back to our senses, but they only reinforced the scientific mentality that has moved us to control the world and lose ourselves.

And now we are taught from earliest childhood to trust instruments more than our own deepest feelings. We are encouraged to view as true that which is most removed from our own persons. This mode of being finds its polar opposite in the richness and intensity of traditional Eastern thought, which is scientific in another way: if only the individual will find and emulate a good teacher, and follow specific steps, then he will certainly know the Divine Ground, the repository of all truths, by a direct intuition superior to discursive reasoning. But this also tends toward imbalance, because the individual becomes too easily passive, careless of the Divine Ground as manifested in the common matter and energy of our daily world.

For me, aikido balances the extremes. It offers contemplation and transcendence. It is also active and effective. In the ordered interplay between the individual and the world, between the nage and the uke, it allows us to check out theory against action, and perhaps to return the human body to realms from which it has long been absent.

IDEAL FORMS. "Perfection exists. You already know these techniques. I'm here only to remind you." In the matter of ideal forms, my teacher, Robert Nadeau, is an unconscious Platonist. The concept of an immaterial reality informs all his teaching. Nadeau assumes, however, that incorporeal being can be approached through bodily consciousness rather than through conceptions alone.

The shiho-nage (four-way throw) is a particularly beautiful and rather difficult aikido technique. One version of it involves grasping the uke's attacking hand with both of your hands, moving to his side, then spinning so that his hand is brought over your head, thus behind his back. From this position, the uke is easily thrown backward to the mat. Performing the necessary turn while remaining upright and centered can be a tricky matter. Rather than teaching this maneuver piecemeal, Nadeau asks us to meditate on the idea of the perfect turn. This turn, he tells us, already exists at the uke's side. We may think of it as a whirlpool, already spinning there. Once we have this idea firmly in our minds and bodies (and for Nadeau the two are not separate) all we have to do is move to the uke's side, into the whirlpool, into the perfect turn. Everything else—balance, centering, posture, feet, arms, hands—will take care of itself.

We are Americans and pragmatic. Will it *work*? We give it a try and find that Nadeau is right. The shiho-nage flows most smoothly when the reality of the *idea* is fixed firmly in the consciousness, and no analysis is needed.

The same thing is true of every aikido movement. For example, if the nage resorts to physical force in a certain wristlock, he may bring a stronger attacker down, but only with much muscular effort. Nadeau suggests an ideal form: energy pouring out through the arm and hand, streaming over the uke's wrist like a waterfall, then flowing from the nage's fingers down to the center of the earth. The uke goes down like a shot without the use of any perceptible physical effort. The difference is startling.

Nadeau's teaching methods run counter to the prevailing direction of most physical education and coaching. The physical education experts continue their work of breaking down every skill into smaller and smaller fragments, analyzing every movement and submovement with the help of film, computers advanced mechanics, and math. Nadeau finds this obsession with analysis rather amusing. It may help well-coached athletes achieve step-by-step improvements, but it can't bring forth the quantum leaps in human functioning that he feels are possible. Nadeau also questions the prevailing view that specific physical skills are nontransferable. The experts feel that years spent perfecting the kick may do little or nothing to improve the pass. For Nadeau, the essence of one physical movement is transferable to every physical movement. "Most of aikido," he says, "can be taught in one simple, blending movement." What is more, the principles learned in aikido should influence the way you play golf, drive, talk to your children, work at your job, make love—the way you live.

CAUSALITY. What makes things happen? Our particular brand of common sense has a ready answer. The cue ball moves because I strike it with the cue. The seven ball moves because the cue hits it. The attacker falls because I throw him down. It is hard for us to escape the concept Aristotle categorized as "efficient causation." We insist on linking our every action to the chain of necessary cause and effect. Unthinking, we conceive ourselves as creatures who go about the world making things happen without ourselves being changed. This assumption, however you look at it, seems rather naïve. Some two centuries ago, Hume showed that what we call causality is only a measure of subjective expectation. Temporal succession means that A regularly precedes B in time, but does not prove the necessity of cause-and-effect linkage. The Positivists tried to explain the succession of events in terms of a purely objective relative frequency.

In aikido, it is much simpler. Just at the perfect movement *already exists,* each perceived event, even one in which we "do" something, is *already happening.* There is a flow in the universe. Our task is to join it.

The Way abides in nonaction,
Yet nothing is left undone.

If Lao-tzu's *Tao Te Ching* seems to offer only paradox on this matter, it is perhaps a good measure of our minds' present limitations. Body and being in action resolve the paradox. Sometimes, even as a relative novice, I can perceive the fields, the flow, the rhythm of the universe. I am part of the universe. The uke is part of the universe. When he attacks me, my body, my arms, and hands, follow a motion that already is happening. There is no waiting, no goal, no *doing.*

Yet nothing is left undone. In these delightful moments, the thrower is not separate from the thrown. We blend in a single motion, a small ripple in an endless sea of existence.

HARMONY. UNITY. All sorts of people come to our dojo—tired businessmen, newly divorced men and women, aging actors and actresses, street people, entrepreneurs of the spirit, new converts to Women's Liberation, experts in other martial arts. There is no beginning, no end. We all step on the mat together, the first-time curiosity seeker along with the dedicated third-degree black belt. We bow, then kneel in the Japanese meditation position around the edges of the mat. In a world of organized hostility and random violence, a world that preaches competition and practices paranoia, we seek universal harmony and the unity of all existence.

Many people come only for a few sessions. Some drop out when they realize they will receive from aikido no violent instrument for their anger. Others are looking for something sequential—progress, "graduation." They cannot grasp the notion of a lifelong journey with no fixed destination. We regulars move about with those who come and go, all of us teachers, all students. Feet get tangled up. Attackers veer off course. On our mat we can see every wound inflicted by our present civilization. The angst, alienation, and anomie of our times appear clearly in the motion of an arm, in the quality of the energy field that surrounds a movement.

And yet, crippled and blind, we eventually begin to sense the *harmonia* that burst upon Pythagoras as a revelation of the whole cosmic system. Behind the curtain of our imperfections there lies the geometry of the humming strings. No matter that we are all different. No matter that our art is built on defense against physical attack. "That which opposes fits," Heraclitus tells us. "Different elements make the finest harmony." We are summer and winter, day and night, smooth and rough, attacker and defender. We are, just possibly, harmony.

There is a sort of dance we often use as a warm-up. Two of us stand facing each other. In three turning steps we pass, face to face, almost touching. We end facing each other again; we have merely changed sides. We repeat the movement again and again, a hundred times, a thousand times. Eventually we can feel that we really are one, a single organism. We are yin and yang, restating our interchangeability. We are a magnet shifting polarity; there is a *click* as we pass, a change in the current. The surface differences between us smooth out. Our bodies tingle. We settle into the eternal present, at home in the universe.

It is said that Pythagoras was the first to call the world *cosmos,* a word that is hard for us to translate, since it contains the ideas of both perfect order and intense beauty. By studying *cosmos,* the Pythagoreans believed, we reproduce it in our own souls. Through philosophy, we assimilate some of the divine within our own bodies. In aikido practice, we simply turn this belief around. Through the experience of our bodies, we come to know *cosmos.*

MULTIPLICITY. Bodies that change size and shape. A manipulable ethereal body superimposed on the physical body. A mysterious inner weight or "true gravity" that the adept can shift at will. Such notions of multiple being within ultimate unity offend the mind of the West, which clings rather desperately to what Blake called "single vision." And yet, multiplicity is central to Oriental thought and to the mystical tradition of all cultures. The Hindu Upanishads describe five koshas, or "soul sheaths," of which the physical body is only one. Indian philosophy in general has much to say about the sukshma shariria, the so-called "subtle," or "feeling," body. In the Western tradition, the Neoplatonists conceived a subtle body and a radiant body, though you won't hear about this in your run-of-the-mill philosophy class.

Our training in Aikido calls for no theoretical study. From the beginning, we realize the multiplicity of perception and being through direct experience. Robert Nadeau in no way denies the reality of the physical body with its bones, blood, muscles, and the like. But he offers us other resources. By sensing the flow of ki (life energy), we can create a powerful yet relaxed "energy arm" in and around the physical arm, so that the arm, however you wish to conceive it, becomes virtually unbendable. By making parts of the energy body smaller, we can slip out of a grasp. By lowering our center of gravity and sending a flow of ki down into earth, we can become seemingly much heavier. At one public demonstration, my daughter, at one hundred ten pounds, moved her ki energy downward so effectively that a weight lifter was unable to budge her. The Western mind rushes for a rational explanation. Mutual hypnotism? That's one way of talking about it. But recent studies in hypnotism have shown that the term is a loose one. In any case, as we'll see in the next chapter, even the most reductive explanation cannot entirely reduce experience.

Simply by considering possibilities commonly ignored or covertly forbidden by our culture, we find ourselves in a far more fascinating universe. We discover adventures that do not require the burning of fuel or the rape of the planet: sensing the energy field of a friend or a tree, making connections that defy conventional space and time, traveling across dazzling new vistas of perception and being. We realize, with the sorcerer don Juan, that our world is "awesome, mysterious, and unfathomable" and that our life is filled to the brim and altogether too short.

Like most of us, I retain a measure of skepticism, sometimes denying my own experience in favor of the artificial cognitive structure erected by this faltering civilization. But I know now that there are other voices, other realities. We sometimes practice Aikido techniques while wearing blindfolds, and I am learning that there is a kind of seeing for which the eyes must be closed. Perhaps I can remain agnostic but not blind, skeptical but not so arrogant as to rule out everything my instruments can measure. "The end of the method of the Pythagorean," wrote the fifth-century Neoplatonic philosopher Hierocles, "was that they should become furnished with wings to soar to the reception of the divine blessings, in order that, when the day of death comes, the Athletes in the Games of Philosophy, leaving the mortal body on earth and stripping off its nature, may be unencumbered for the heavenly journey."

VIRTUE. In Aikido, as in Plato and in the perennial mystical tradition, virtue is not an end in itself, but the indispensable means to the knowledge of the Good or of divine reality. In his memoir, Master Morihei Ueshiba wrote: "The secret of Aikido is to harmonize ourselves with the movement of the universe and bring ourselves into accord with the universe itself. He who has gained the secret of Aikido has the universe in himself and can say, 'I am the universe.'" This universal harmony, it seems to me, stands as the ultimate Good in Aikido. According to Ueshiba, "This is not mere theory. You practice it. Then you will accept the great power of oneness with Nature. Virtue is practice, the steady, disciplined practice of loving attack and peaceful reconciliation."

My teacher, in a radical, ultimately Christian application of virtue in practice, asks us not to master but to serve the attacker. It's up to us to be so sensitive to the attacker's intentions and needs (whether the attack be physical or mental) that we know precisely where he wants to go and what he wants to do. Blending with him, and taking ourselves slightly out of harm's way, we can help the attacker do what he intends. Somewhere, at the completion of the act, there is a point at which he rejoins the harmony of nature. Every attacker is destined, in any case, to take a fall.

Of course, if each of us were to be totally sensitive to the needs and intentions of all those around us, there would be no attacks.

HEAVEN AND EARTH. Perhaps the loveliest of aikido techniques is called tenchi-nage (heaven and earth throw). As in all aikido techniques, the tenchi-nage occurs in many variations, but always involves one arm being raised upward, the other reaching down. In this manner, the attacker's strength and intentions are split between heaven and earth, and there is nothing for him to do—until his moment of reconciliation—but fall.

I am practicing one variation of tenchi-nage. My technique is uncertain. Because I am uncertain, I am rough. I throw down my uke with unnecessary force. This is not aikido. On this occasion the uke is Tom Everett. In his early twenties, Everett is an accomplished aikidoist.

"Let's start again," he suggests. "What qualities do you associate with heaven?"
"Heaven? Clouds, lightness, angels."
"And earth?"
"Solidity, weight, massiveness."
"All right. One of your arms is heaven. The other is earth." He laughs. "It's simple."
I spend a moment investing my arms with these qualities.
"Don't think about technique," Everett reminds me. "Just heaven and earth."
And it is simple, if only because I have been led to the right questions.

In the end, every historical period appears to us not in terms of the answers it provides but of the questions it asks. In a period that glorifies "combativeness," from the first physical education class to the last television show, our major questions become conflict-ridden. For example, Norman Mailer, speaking for a significant proportion of our literary-intellectual culture, leads us to believe that the most significant question we can ask of the space program, and most other things as well, is whether it is the work of God or the devil. It is a question for which there seems to be no satisfactory answer. In the same way, the old culture clings to this romantic dualism, to Aristotelian categorization, to the "tragic vision," to the "human condition." Is it possible that we are coming to the end of this kind of thinking?

In a remarkable essay, "New Heaven, New Earth," Joyce Carol Oates writes:

> We are satiated with the "objective," valueless philosophies that have always worked to preserve a status quo, however archaic. We are tired of the old dichotomies: Sane/Insane, Normal/Sick, Black/White, Man/Nature, Victor/Vanquished, and above all this Cartesian dualism—I/It. Although once absolutely necessary to get us through the exploratory, analytical phase of our development as human beings, they are no longer useful or pragmatic. They are no longer *true* . . . What appears to be a breaking down of civilization may well be simply the breaking down of old forms by life itself (not an eruption of madness or self-destruction), a process that is entirely natural and inevitable . . . . The death throes of the old values are everywhere around us, but they are not the same thing as the death throes of particular human beings. We can transform ourselves.

If such a change is indeed upon us, we need balance and harmony, sensitivity and the art of reconciliation—not ego, the test of manhood, the clash of force against force, the battle of God versus the devil. The secret of tenchi-nage is that the separation between heaven and earth is only apparent. Ultimately they are one. In Lao-tzu's words:

> The space between heaven and earth is like a bellows.
> The shape changes but not the form;
> The more it moves, the more it yields.

When my practice goes well, I am, if only for a short while, one with the universe. Within the one are heaven and earth and much more—not only friends and lovers but also the convict in solitary confinement, the dread enemy in the jungle—all part of me, all part of us. The time has come to ask about reconciliation, which starts not at some distant place, but here, in my body and being, and in yours.

THE MEANING OF "AI," "KI", "DO"
By Wayne F. Tourda

AI: Adaptability

Everything in nature is in a state of flux. Nothing is ever the same except change. It is the only constant. We have a choice between trying to resist this change or accepting it by becoming harmonious with it. Life is about adaptability, whether it be physical or psychological. Therefore we are constantly adapting to our environment.

KI: The essence of our being

In the martial arts, the Japanese word *ki* refers to our innermost nature or the deepest core within our being, which is in union with the universe. It is what we were before our parents were born or before they met. It is what we will be after we move through this life cycle, which consists of five simple yet difficult steps: life, birth, growth, decay, death. *Ki* has often been referred to as *prana*, breath, spirit, or *chi.* It is that from which we came and is that to which we must return.

DO: The way

If we are so fortunate as to survive the pressures of conformity to the five basic institutions—family, religion, education, government, business—the individual path of self-perfection will at times reveal itself. This venture is by no means an easy path, but the reward is significant. The light at the end of the tunnel will no longer be the train coming at you; it is *truly* the light at the end of the tunnel.

To retrieve a tiger's cub you must enter the tiger's den.

Zen saying

THE HISTORY OF AIKIDO AND ITS FOUNDER

By John J. Donahue

Morihei Ueshiba, the founder of Aikido, was born on December 18, 1883. An examination of the course of Ueshiba's life underscores the essentially religious nature of his quest for direction. Since Aikido is perhaps the most spiritually oriented of modern budo, his fundamentally spiritual quest is significant. Aikido, as a philosophic *and* physical system, is the culmination of Ueshiba's life experience.

Ueshiba was a sickly child who was more interested in the rites of Esoteric Buddhism than he was in the swimming and sumo lessons his father forced upon him. While demonstrating no lack of ability, Ueshiba was a restless youth. His early life showed a pattern of incessant searching for a satisfying life goal, often brought to a head by a physical or psychological crisis, following which Ueshiba would embark on a new and different pursuit. Although training in the martial arts formed an early constant in Ueshiba's life and served to improve his health, it was to assume importance only after the age of thirty.

His chronic restlessness as a young man caused him to leave middle school after only one year. Obtaining a position in the government tax office, Ueshiba resigned in righteous indignation over what he considered to be unfair tax policies. In 1901, he went to Tokyo with the goal of establishing himself as a businessman. His small office supplies store folded after only a few months. While a resounding failure as merchant, it was in Tokyo that Ueshiba began his study of Kito Ryu jujutsu and Shinkage Ryu swordsmanship. As Ueshiba's business collapsed around him, however, he became ill, and so returned home to Tanabe.

After a period of recuperation, Ueshiba enlisted in the Army in 1903. A lack of formal education prevented him from obtaining an officer's commission, which might have been a goal consistent with his personality and his growing interest in the martial arts. He served with distinction during the Russo-Japanese War of 1904-05 and eventually rose to the rank of sergeant. During his period of enlistment he gained his *menkyo* (teaching license) in a form of jujutsu that evolved from the techniques of the Yagyu Ryu. Despite a relatively successful career in the military and encouragement from his superiors to stay, Ueshiba's restless spirit impelled him to resign from the armed forces in 1907.

He once again returned home to Tanabe but was at a loss to decide what to do. He prowled the small town, restless, irritable, "almost manic depressive" and engaged in a series of wild and irrational acts: fasting and praying in the mountains late at night, and locking himself in his room for hours. His father, at a loss as to how to help his son, had a jujutsu dojo constructed on his property in the hopes that such physical activity would help Ueshiba. The practice of the martial arts did indeed have a positive effect on Ueshiba's character, and his behavior became much less extreme.

To a certain extent, though, Ueshiba's restlessness remained. In 1912, he and a number of other villagers volunteered to pioneer a wilderness area of Hokkaido, the northernmost and least settled area in Japan. In the new settlement of Shirataki, Ueshiba, his family, and neighbors labored at logging and farming. Ueshiba's extreme physical fitness (the result of untold hours spent in the dojo) and abundant energy found positive outlets in the demanding physical environment of Hokkaido, and he became a prominent member of the fledgling communities around Shirataki.

His move to Hokkaido did not spell an end to Ueshiba's martial training. In terms of the development of Aikido, the Hokkaido period in Ueshiba's life was vitally important, for here, in 1915, he met Takeda Sogaku, master of Daito Ryu Aiki-jutsu. The techniques of Aiki-jutsu proved a revelation to Ueshiba, and he undertook their study with a vengeance. By 1917, he was accompanying Takeda on trips as a teaching assistant.

The physical methods of the Daito Ryu were consequently elaborated on and refined by Ueshiba and were to form the technical base upon which he built his system of Aikido. From a technical standpoint, many of the principles and techniques of Aiki-jutsu are similar to those incorporated into Kano's eclectic system of judo. There are, however, numerous points of difference between the two. For one thing, Aiki techniques are more often circular in motion. Instead of the "push when pulled, pull when pushed" theory of judo, Aiki emphasizes circular motions which serve to dissipate the opponent's energy.

Ueshiba's move to Hokkaido also did not mark the end of his interest in religion. It was in Hokkaido, in fact, that he became interested in the Omoto-kyo sect of Shinto. Then, in 1919, Ueshiba was informed that his father, who had remained in Tanabe, was seriously ill. On his way south to see his ailing parent, Ueshiba stopped at the headquarters of Omoto-kyo in the town of Ayabe. Entranced, he lingered there for three days. On arriving in Tanabe, Ueshiba was devastated to learn that, while he tarried at the Omoto-kyo headquarters, his father had passed away. This event precipitated another crisis in Ueshiba's life. After his father's death, Ueshiba hardly ate or slept for three months. His behavior once again became increasingly irrational, and every night he would take to the mountains and swing his sword madly until daybreak. Finally, he announced to his family his decision to sell off the ancestral land in Tanabe and join the Omoto-kyo sect. This sudden and dramatic decision came after a series of personal tragedies. Between 1919 and 1920 Ueshiba had lost his father and two infant sons. Family friends worried that the series of tragedies had driven Ueshiba insane. Nonetheless, Ueshiba would not be swayed, and he, his wife and their young daughter moved to Ayabe and immersed themselves in the life of Omoto-kyo.

Ueshiba was deeply affected by the eight years he spent in Ayabe. From 1921 to 1929, he studied the religious principles of Omoto-kyo and actively pursued a deeper understanding of budo. Ueshiba established a dojo, the Ueshiba Juku, and had Takeda, the master of Aiki-jutsu, visit him there. At Ayabe, the two central forces in Ueshiba's life, Omoto-kyo and Aiki-jutsu, met and interacted with one another. Ueshiba himself said that Daito Ryu Aiki-jutsu opened his eyes to the essence of budo, while Omoto-kyo was instrumental in leading him to enlightenment. Thus, despite its grounding in traditional combat techniques, *the evolving orientation of Aikido was a spiritual one.*

At first glance, it may seem strange that a pacifist spiritual tradition and a form of unarmed combat should have existed side by side at Ayabe. For Ueshiba, however, many of the doctrines of Omoto-kyo had concrete expression in his budo training, in much the same way that the precepts of Zen had proved so instrumental in the training of feudal bushi.

The Omoto-kyo belief of "calming the spirit and returning to the divine" had an obvious relation in Ueshiba's mind to the development of an outlook that stressed the fundamental spiritual unity of both attacker and defender. For Ueshiba, the emphasis in budo should always be on defense. *Ueshiba modified the essentially aggressive techniques of Aiki-jutsu into a system that was not concerned with conflict but with creating harmony between the Aiki adept and the antagonist. In Ueshiba's opinion, it was only as a basically defensive art that budo had any moral justification.*

Ueshiba saw all sentient beings as existing in unity. Therefore, all beings, including aggressors, were entitled to protection and loving care. Ueshiba's ideas developed into an extension of the idea of "transcending subject-object distinctions." What had, for the early samurai, been a philosophical tool for the improvement of their martial technique was now developed into a moral rationale for the practice of a certain type of budo. Thus, *Ueshiba's budo developed an essentially spiritual goal which was articulated through physical techniques: the constant training of mind and body for human beings walking the spiritual path.*

Ueshiba's very strong conviction concerning the need for universal love is by no means a unique one in the annals of human thought. Although not a dominant strain in Eastern philosophy, we note such concepts appearing as early as the fifth century B.C. in China, embodied in the teachings of the philosopher Mo-Tzu. What is unique in this instance is Ueshiba's link of such a philosophy with the pursuit of a martial discipline. Swordsmen like Yagyu Munenori had, of course, attempted to emphasize the moral duty of the bushi, and this trend was especially notable during the Tokugawa era. However, Ueshiba's call to love the aggressor and render him powerless by the power of affection, as expressed through the techniques of Aiki, was unique.

BUDO (Martial Way)

By Wayne F. Tourda

BUDO is dedicated to perfecting the human self by integrating mind, body, and spirit. The training and discipline consist of three levels of mastery: physical, psychological, and spiritual.

On the physical level, mastery of form is the crux of training. The teacher provides a model form; the student observes carefully and repeats it countless times until he has completely internalized the form. Few words are spoken and few explanations are given; the burden of learning is on the student. In the ultimate mastery of form, the student is released from adherence to form.

This release occurs because of internal psychological changes taking place from the very beginning. The tedious, repetitious, and monotonous learning routine tests the student's commitment and will power, but it also reduces stubbornness, curbs willfulness, and eliminates bad habits of body and mind.

The spiritual mastery is inseparable from the psychological, but begins only after an intensive and lengthy period of training. Ultimately, physical, psychological, and spiritual mastery are one and the same. The individual becomes open, flexible, supple, fluid, and dynamic in body, mind, and spirit. While many people may fall short of this goal, the crucial element is the process of training, which is without beginning and without end.

Source: Kisshomaru Ueshiba's The Spirit of Aikido

THE DISTINCTION AMONG CLASSICAL AIKIJUTSU, CLASSICAL BUDO (AIKIDO), AND MODERN AIKIDO

By Wayne F. Tourda

As change is the only constant in the universe, nowhere do we see this evolutionary process more clearly than in the martial arts. Hence, once again, we are embroiled in the great change. As feudalism began to reach its demise and the world became smaller with the advent of modern weaponry, the question became, how can we continue to train ourselves in a somewhat more civilized society? The answer was that *we* had to change. As we see in charts 1 and 2, classical aikijutsu's primary objective had been to destroy for self-defense. In classical budo (aikido), on the other hand, self-defense became secondary in importance. However, this evolutionary process began to reach its zenith only in the late 1920's, when O Sensei founded modern-day Aikido.

It is this final step in the evolutionary process that we as martial artists began to understand: that love is stronger than hate, that soft is stronger than hard, that giving is stronger than taking, and that winning by losing can be an admirable accomplishment. While self-defense is still important, it is now only a by-product in modern Aikido.

Suppleness has the power to turn nature against itself.

Zen saying

Classical Bujutsu	Classical Budo (Aikido)
↓ End: Classical Warrior (Eternally Combat-Ready) ↓ Training Methods ↓ Traits (Means to an End) ↓ Classical Warrior	↓ End: Traits of Classical Warrior ↓ Training Methods ↓ Traits (Ends in Themselves) ↓ Effective Warrior (By Product) (efficient and effective in practical situations)

Classical Bujutsu (Aikijutsu)	Classical Budo (Aikido)	Modern Budo (Aikido)
• Focused • Energetic • Decisive • Courageous • Alert • Forward Moving • Flexible • Discerning (Discreat) • Mindful • Unselfish • Committed to something beyond oneself • Clarity of Mind • Self-Disciplined • Unconquerable Spirit • Willing and able to suffer for the higher goal • Destroys only what needs to be destroyed (corruption, oppression, injustice)	• Focused • Energetic • Decisive • Courageous • Alert • Forward Moving • Flexible • Discerning (Discreat) • Mindful • Committed to something beyond oneself • Clarity of Mind • Self-Disciplined • Unconquerable Spirit • Willing and able to suffer for the higher goal • Destroys only what needs to be destroyed (corruption, oppression, injustice) • Cooperative • Giving • Unselfish • Helpful • Flexible Mind • Humble Spirit	• Cooperative • Giving • Unselfish • Helpful • Flexible Mind • Humble Spirit

Modern Bujutsu (Aikijutsu)	Modern Budo (Aikido)
End: Self-Defense Techniques	End: More Harmonious Life /Harmony with Nature

Classical Bujutsu (Aikijutsu) → Classical Budo (Aikido)
Techniques Changed
Training methods are the same (more severe - demanding)

Classical Bujutsu (Aikijutsu) ↓ Modern Bujitsu (Aikijutsu):
Training Methods Change
Techniques Same

Classical Budo (Aikido) ↓ Modern Budo (Aikido):
Training Methods Change
Techniques Same

Modern Bujitsu (Aikijutsu) → Modern Budo (Aikido)
Techniques Changed
Training methods are the same (in the sense that they are both less severe (demanding) than the classical methods.)

IN BUDO, WE LOOK WITHIN TO FIND THE ANSWERS

By Dave Lowry

"When the superior man fails to hit the target with his arrow," noted Confucius, "he looks for faults not in his bow, but in himself."

When the early Western archer found limitations in his skills, he responded by improving technology, fashioning better bows. When the Japanese archer encountered boundaries in his shooting ability, he responded by improving himself. This comparison is a bit over-simplistic, but it does acknowledge a fundamental difference in the thinking of West and East, one that has considerable influences on the budo (martial ways) and the way they are approached in Japanese and American dojo (training halls).

A state-of-the-art bow in the West today is a weapon of space-age polymers, outfitted with pulleys, telescopic sights and string-vibration suppressors. The bow a modern deer hunter uses would be unrecognizable to the North American Stone Age Indian, but look at a modern Japanese yumi (bow) and you will see virtually the same weapon the samurai used to shoot arrows on the 14th-century battlefield. It has a core of laminations of sumac wood and bamboo, and its shape and length have been fixed for many generations. There have been no improvements to speak of in the technology of Japanese archery in several hundred years. Two civilizations, yet two very different ways of approaching the same instrument.

Typically when a Westerner was introduced to the martial arts, he was reluctant to accept them at face value. And he probably never even considered doing so. Before long, he was busily making what he believed were "improvements."

The real challenge of making improvements in the budo is not whether these changes are good or bad – they can be both. The essence of the matter is in recognizing when such progress is merely a diversion from the martial path. There comes a time when the budoka must realize the limitations of technologies, and when he must understand and act upon the Confucian notion that he himself is responsible for his refinement in the dojo. If you are struggling with a technique you can work with the weights, read books and watch video tapes. It is a hallmark of our age that such things are in profusion to assist – *and tempt* – us. Yet, in the end, we must, like the archer, turn to ourselves. We must practice the technique perfecting it as we do ourselves.

To me, one of the most appealing and profound aspects of the budo is that they allow those who pursue them all sorts of diversions and do nothing to keep you from going off in pursuit of this or that. And in the end, they will be waiting, unchanged, for you to return to the correct and original path. When the technique doesn't feel right, the technique won't work. You can look to technology for the answer, but sooner or later, you'll have to look within yourself.

THE SEVEN PRINCIPLES OF BUDO
By Wayne F. Tourda

GI (RECTITUDE): The right decision taken with equanimity; the power of resolution – of deciding upon a certain course of conduct without wavering.

YU (COURAGE): Perceiving what is right, and doing it not, argues lack of courage.

JIN (BENEVOLENCE): Compassion toward mankind; a benevolent person is ever mindful of those who are suffering and in distress.

REI (COURTESY): The outward manifestation of a sympathetic regard for the feelings of others; courtesy would be a great acquisition if it did no more than impart grace to manners. But its function does not stop here. For propriety, springing as it does from motives of benevolence and modesty, and actuated by tender feelings toward the sensibilities of others, is a graceful expression of sympathy.

MAKOTO (SINCERITY): Sincerity denotes honesty, both with oneself and with others. Sincerity also denotes purity of motive, a rejection of self-serving, "practical" objectives, and complete moral fastidiousness. The sincere warrior always placed means before ends and all that mattered was that he acted out of a selfless purity of principle.

MEYLO (HONOR): A vivid consciousness of personal dignity and worth.

CHUGO (DEVOTION, LOYALTY): Homage and fealty to one's seniors.

Sources: Deshimaru's The Zen Way to the Martial Arts;.Nitobe's Bushido: The Soul of Japan;

ON COURTESY AND BUDO

By Wayne F. Tourda

In The Zen Way of the Martial Arts, Taisen Deshimaru says the following about courtesy, or *rei*:

> The outward manifestation of a sympathetic regard for the feelings of others; courtesy would be a great acquisition if it did no more than impart grace to manners. But its function does not stop here. For propriety, springing as it does from motives of benevolence and modesty, and actuated by tender feelings toward the sensibilities of others, is a graceful expression of sympathy."

Aikido begins and ends with courtesy and etiquette. From the moment we enter the dojo, we bow to the front to create an overall respect to something or someone greater than ourselves. Unfortunately, many westerners have difficulty with the practice of bowing as a result of an uncontrolled ego. It is this very ego which must be dropped in order for us to make harmony as practitioners of the art.

At the beginning of class, everyone including the instructor faces the front and by bowing shows respect for the wonderful opportunity to study together, after which time the instructor turns to face the senior student and in effect thanks him for helping him help the students. Throughout the entire class a continuous feeling of gratitude towards our fellow students in the way of etiquette and decorum is demonstrated, thereby producing a sense of community among the students.

It is most important to remember that this sense of courtesy and decorum must be practiced not only on the mat but in daily life. This can only be accomplished by throwing out the self or ego. The first step in improving the world begins with improving ourselves. This is the goal of our training.

Possessions possess.

Zen saying

PHILOSOPHICAL IDEAS IN MARTIAL ARTS TRAINING
By Herman Kauz

In the East, it is not unusual for people to think of the study of a martial art as training for living life.

Relevant ideas from Taoism, Buddhism, and Confucianism were incorporated into the philosophy of the martial arts as they developed through the centuries. Of course, these ideas found their way into, and in another sense underlay, everything that was done in the Eastern societies. However, teachers of disciplines such as the martial arts usually attempted to originate training methods that would enable their students to directly apprehend the content or spirit of some of these philosophical concepts. Their intention was to help students understand important truths intuitively, to develop their insight, rather than to have contact with these ideas only intellectually.

Although the emphasis in martial arts is usually on practice rather than on philosophical speculation, teachers will sometimes speak of philosophical concepts which underlie their instruction. Also, an examination of the administrative or hierarchical structure and the teaching method of a school readily reveal the presence of various elements of Asian philosophical doctrine. Of course, one art might stress certain ideas more than might another. But in general, the following six ideas will be present in varying degrees:

Respect for life and Nature: A belief that we are part of Nature and should attempt to live harmony with it rather than manipulate it to serve our ends alone. In addition, we should learn to cultivate and preserve life and avoid its destruction. More specifically, in training we are taught to avoid injuring our partner. We are asked to be gentle and helpful to those weaker than ourselves. If we are forced to use our art to defend ourselves or those around us, we should do so with utmost restraint. Our intention should always be to avoid injuring an attacker if a less extreme method of defense will safely turn aside his attack. Unfortunately, such discretion demands a high degree of skill as well as an unusual concern for the welfare of others. If threatened with injury or worse, even a trained martial artist will seldom employ halfway measures to meet an attack once it has actually been launched. Thus, every effort must be made to avoid an attack before it is expressed physically.

Wu wei or non-action: The idea that the various systems in Nature are interdependent and that the world will function best if we refrain from disturbing one part or another in order to improve the whole. This concept is clearly related to the foregoing one. Action that interferes with Nature's functioning is to be avoided at the risk of incurring disaster. However, action taken in accordance with Nature's course is justified and necessary. In martial arts, this concept might take the form of helping the body to relax by using certain exercises designed to better enable its natural functioning to proceed unimpeded by tension. This might be reflected in training by not resisting an opponent's attack. The use of this tactic theoretically results in the attacker losing his balance because he has overextended in the direction of the target he mistakenly thought was solid. In this way, we use the opponent's strength to defeat him; or it might be said that by attacking he defeats himself.

Moderation and Balance: An avoidance of over-or under-extension in any direction. Attempting in whatever we do, to go far enough, but also not to go too far. As with *wu wei*, this concept in martial arts might take the form of avoiding the use of an excessive degree of strength or energy in order to accomplish an attacking or defending maneuver. But it also demands the employment of sufficient energy to achieve a desired result.

Education for training character: The idea that the subject matter a student studies and the method by which he is taught is employed primarily to develop his character. The intention of the teacher is first and foremost to turn out superior personnel who would be considered "good" or "worthy" in their particular culture. Knowledge of subject matter would be important as well, but would be secondary. In martial arts, many teachers look upon their calling as a method through which they help students bring about beneficial change in themselves. Often such change is thought to take the form of learning to withstand adversity, of not giving in when things are going badly. However, such stoicism is combined with other traits, such as helping the weak, mentioned above, in an effort to produce strong but gentle persons. These teachers are not concerned primarily with training fighters, although their students usually demonstrate considerable technical skill.

Filial piety and conformity to the social order: The filial piety learned in a family in which children respect and obey their parents, and younger brothers those who are older, is carried over into society in the form of respect for authority, and, above all, proper conduct or propriety. This is not a one-way street, however, since those in a superior position also have their obligations to those below them. This pattern in martial arts lends itself to a hierarchical structure in which the teacher stands at the top of a pyramid with senior students on the level below him and beginners at the bottom. A teacher receives the respect and loyalty of his students, in effect taking the role of the father in the "family" formed by the martial arts school. Senior students assume the role of older brothers. In addition, certain rules of etiquette are strictly observed within the training hall. For example, students might be asked to demonstrate respect for their training by bowing to the practice area as they arrive and when they leave. They might be required to sit in a particular way. Interaction with fellow students and with the teacher might have to follow prescribed pattern.

Transcendental spirit and enlightenment: The concern here is with spiritual development. Generally speaking, for Chinese philosophers, this does not necessitate a retreat from the world. Rather, the external environment, which we experience each day, provides a means to gain insight into the working of the world and man's place in the scheme of things. Another consideration, or perhaps a way of describing this insight, is enlightenment. Esoteric training methods have been used for centuries to help students penetrate beyond the surface appearance of things and events. Various forms of meditation are perhaps the most important of these methods. The martial arts can be taught with primary emphasis on their meditative character. Those martial arts teachers with the requisite skill in this area do what they can to help students penetrate their self-created veil of illusion about themselves and the world.

It might be useful to round out the above discussion with a more detailed picture of the teaching method at a school of martial arts in which elements of Zen Buddhism are present. If we accept the premise that the teacher's intention at such a school is to help his students see themselves and life generally more clearly, we nevertheless may feel that his methods are unnecessarily stern. If our background is of a kind that excludes acquaintance with such methods, we might even regard them as dehumanizing. However, one of the underlying ideas in this kind of training is that if a student is to grow in his understanding of life he must become aware of aspects of himself that seldom come to conscious attention. To get the student to see beyond the surface of things physical and mental, shocks are employed. The teacher's approach can be characterized as an attempt to put students into position where their usual manner of viewing life becomes subject to self-examination.

Put another way, the dominance of the ego over the student's life is questioned. By "ego" is meant the mental symbol we use to identify ourselves in our thinking. As we live our daily lives, we usually hold certain ideas about ourselves based on memory, forgetting that these ideas are just symbols and not our real nature. We are changing constantly. Yet we approach most situations thinking of ourselves as having distinct and fixed qualities of mind and character. We even have fixed ideas about our physical appearance. Becoming conscious of possessing certain physical and non-physical characteristics seems to occur to most of us at some particular time in our lives. When it happens, we tend to become locked into that cluster of ideas and find it difficult to free ourselves. It becomes apparent that our image of ourselves is probably not what we are. Moreover, as time goes by, this image often becomes frozen and no longer changes as we change. As we interact with others, we carry this concealed idea of ourselves into each situation. What is happening must somehow conveniently fit this image or the image must be able to fit into what happens. As a consequence, we become unable to react to each situation as if it were fresh and new, which it is. We attempt to make it immediately into something we may have previously encountered and responded to with some degree of success. On the other hand, we may respond to it negatively, believing it resembles other situations in which we have failed or performed inadequately. Either manner of relating to life leaves little room for spontaneity or for being open enough to see what is really happening. It contributes to inflexibility of mind and a reluctance to try something new.

A teacher of martial arts who holds such views about the way most people's minds work, and who believes this state of affairs is unhealthy, will begin to help the student to see himself in a different way. To accomplish this he will probably subject the student's ego to constant attack.

The road along which beginners are guided is one marked by hard practice and discipline. They receive few opportunities to grasp intellectual handles with which to rationalize their training. Mentally comprehending the subject matter is only the first step on the way to learning. The general overriding concept is that the student must internalize what is being taught and must gradually make it part of himself. To that end he is encouraged to perform repetitious movements either alone or with a partner. As is usual with an attempt to learn something new, he feels inadequate. At first, try as he will, he cannot perform the required movements with the correctness , smoothness, relaxation and seeming total absorption that more advanced students or his teacher demonstrate. Any attempt by the beginner to avoid giving his all to his training is discouraged. Depending upon the art, this discouragement might take the form of especially rigorous treatment at the hands of senior students or the teacher. Attempts to compensate for inadequate performance by recourse to some sort of dialogue is usually treated similarly.

Of course, this method of training presupposes that the beginner has decided to accept the discipline required by his teacher of the art. The student must have faith in his teacher. Looked at in the opposite way, the teacher cannot accept a student's refusal to do things in the prescribed way without severe injury to his whole endeavor. A teacher will usually regard an argumentative student as a person who cannot or will not live up his idea of himself as a certain kind of individual. If matters deteriorate to such a point that a confrontation between student and teacher occurs, the student is usually expelled.

Training for even the most willing student is rigorous and, viewed from a certain perspective, might be termed sadistic. Also, viewed from this perspective, it might be thought that anyone who willingly submits to such treatment has more than the usual amount of masochism in his makeup. But more is at stake here than the everyday relationships of people. The rigorous training is not an end in itself. It is designed to enable the student to experience aspects of himself that usually remain hidden, or that he was unable to see because his prevailing idea of himself obscured his views. He is often pushed beyond the limits he would have chosen for himself, finding that he can go far past the point of apparent physical endurance. He learns about his capabilities under this and related kinds of pressures. Usually he begins to see that he is not what he thought he was, and that when he remembers of himself may well have been inaccurate. Ultimately, he discovers that he functions from a different base than the idea he has of himself, or his ego. He will begin to find that he can approach a situation more openly, allowing it to develop and reacting spontaneously as the necessity for action presents itself.

This approach to training helps move students toward self-realization. At this point the reader might well ask what is meant by the term "self-realization". Perhaps as a general definition we can say that the person who engages in serious martial arts training will be helped to more fully realize his potential as a human being. Certainly he will know more clearly who he is (he will also learn to see his training partners with additional clarity). He will become aware of the strengths and weaknesses of his character. He will learn that sustained application of energy over a long period is the way to get a job done that seems hopeless of accomplishment at first encounter. Thus, he will gain the strength and discipline necessary to further develop aspects of himself which he believes are beneficial and to restrain those he decides are detrimental to his well-being. Finally, he will learn not to give up even when he appears to be in a losing position. Such lessons are invaluable for living life.

The Philosophy

and

Ethics of Aikido

THE PURPOSE OF AIKIDO

A lecture by the Founder, Morihei Ueshiba

I wonder if you grasp the real purpose of Aikido? It is not merely training yourself in the techniques of bujutsu. Its other purpose is the creation of a world of beauty, grace, and elegance. It is to make this world a better place. We have the continued privilege of enjoying its beauty and splendor. It is our obligation, as human beings, to establish a society that does justice to that beauty and splendor. Our goal in budo is not merely to protect ourselves. We must accept the gift of the universal and constantly strive to honor that gift by nurturing the changes that will bring happiness to the world. If we truly honor the sacred heart of budo, we must work for peace, for a world without quarrels, without misery, without conflict. This is the real reason that we practice Aikido. Aikido is a way of making the universal principle clear. The society that harmoniously combines body and mind produces a world of unity. We ourselves must take the responsibility to realize this truth.

Once we are truly aware of the universal plan and its divine purpose, we no longer have any real choice but to apprentice ourselves to the service of this most superb and sacred endeavor. This is the essence and heart of budo, and it is the principal aim of Aikido. When we become aware that our life is a gift from the divine consciousness of the infinite universe, we come to realize our true nature.

A SOFT ANSWER
By Terry Dobson

The train clanked and rattled through the suburbs of Tokyo on a drowsy spring afternoon. At one station the doors opened, and suddenly the afternoon quiet was shattered by a man bellowing violent, incomprehensible curses. The man staggered into our car. He wore laborer's clothing, and he was big, drunk and dirty. Screaming, he swung at a woman holding a baby. The blow sent her spinning into the laps of an elderly couple. It was a miracle that the baby was unharmed.

Terrified, the couple jumped up and scrambled toward the other end of the car. The laborer aimed a kick at the retreating back of the old woman but missed as she scuttled to safety. This so enraged the drunk that he grabbed the metal pole in the center of the car and tried to wrench it out of its stanchion. I could see that one of his hands was cut and bleeding. The train lurched ahead, the passengers frozen with fear. I stood up.

I was young then, some twenty years ago, and in pretty good shape. I'd been putting in a solid eight hours of Aikido training nearly every day for the past three years. I liked to throw and grapple. I thought I was tough. Trouble was, my martial skill was untested in actual combat. As students of Aikido, we were not allowed to fight.

"Aikido," my teacher had said again and again, "is the art of reconciliation. Whoever has the mind to fight has broken his connection with the universe. If you try to dominate people, you are already defeated. We study how to resolve conflict, not how to start it."

I listened to his words, I tried hard. I even went so far as to cross the street to avoid the chimpira, the pinball punks who lounged around the train stations. My forbearance exalted me. I felt both tough and holy. In my heart, however, I wanted an absolutely legitimate opportunity whereby I might save the innocent by destroying the guilty.

This is it! I said to myself as I got to my feet. People are in danger. If I don't do something fast, somebody will probably get hurt.

Seeing me stand up, the drunk recognized a chance to focus his rage, "Ah ha!" he roared. "A foreigner! You need a lesson in Japanese manners!"

I held on lightly to the commuter strap overhead and gave him a slow look of disgust and dismissal. I planned to take this turkey apart, but he had to make the first move. I wanted him mad, so I pursed my lips and blew him an insolent kiss. "All right!" he hollered. "You're gonna get a lesson." He gathered himself for a rush at me.

A split second before he could move someone shouted "Hey!" It was earsplitting. I remember the strangely joyous, lifting quality of it, as though you and a friend has been searching diligently for something and he had suddenly stumbled upon it. "Hey!"

I wheeled to my left; the drunk spun to his right. We both stared down at a little old Japanese. He must have been well into his seventies, this tiny gentleman, sitting there immaculate in his kimono. He took no notice of me but beamed delightedly at the laborer, as though he had the most important, most welcome secret to share.

"C'mere," the old man said in easy vernacular, beckoning to the drunk. "C'mere and talk with me." He waved his hand lightly.

The big man followed, as if on a string. He planted his feet belligerently in front of the old gentleman and roared above the clacking wheels, "Why the held should I talk to you?" The drunk now had his back to me. If the elbow moved so much as a millimeter, I'd drop him in his socks.

The old man continued to beam at the laborer. "What'cha been drinkin?" he asked, his eyes sparkling with interest. "I been drinkin' sake," the laborer bellowed back, "and it's none of your business!" Flecks of spittle spattered the old man.

"Oh, that's wonderful," the old man said, "absolutely wonderful! You see, I love sake too. Every night, me and my wife (she's seventy-six, you know), warm up a little bottle of sake and take it out into the garden, and we sit on an old wooden bench. We watch the sun go down, and we look to see how our persimmon tree is doing. My great-grandfather planted that tree, and we worry about whether it will recover from those ice storms we had last winder. Our tree has done better than I expected, though, especially when you consider the poor quality of soil. It is gratifying to watch when we take our sake and go out to enjoy the evening – even when it rains!" He looked up at the laborer, eyes twinkling.

As he struggled to follow the old man's conversation, the drunk's face began to soften. His fists slowly unclenched. "Yeah," he said, "I love persimmons too…." His voice trailed off.

"Yes," said the old man, smiling. "And I'm sure you have a wonderful wife."

"No," replied the laborer. "My wife died." Very gently, swaying with the motion of the train, the big man began to sob. "I don't got no wife, I don't got no home, I don't got no job. I'm so ashamed of myself." Tears rolled down his cheeks; a spasm of despair rippled through his body.

Now it was my turn. Standing there in my well-scrubbed innocence, my "make this world safe for democracy" righteousness, I suddenly felt dirtier than he was.

Then the train arrived at my stop. As the doors opened I heard the old man cluck sympathetically. "My, my," he said. "That is a difficult predicament, indeed. Sit down here and tell me about it." I turned my head for one last look. The laborer was sprawled on the seat, his head in the old man's lap, the old man softly stroking the filthy, matted hair.

As the train pulled away, I sat down on a bench. What I had wanted to do with muscle had been accomplished with kind words. I had just seen Aikido, tried in combat, and the essence of it was love. I would have to practice the art with an entirely different spirit. It would be a long time before I could speak about the resolution of conflict.

Zen and Aikido

THE NOBLE STRUGGLE OF THE WARRIOR
By Taisen Deshimaru

Budo is the way of the warrior; it embraces all the Japanese martial arts. It explores through direct experience and in depth the relationship between ethics, religion, and philosophy. Its association with sports is a very recent development; the ancient writings are essentially concerned with a particular form of cultivation of the mind and a reflection upon the nature of the self: who am I? *What* is I?

In Japanese, *do* means the way. How do you walk on this way? How can you find it? It is not just learning a technique, still less is it a sporting match. Budo includes such arts as *kendo, judo, aikido,* and *kyudo* or archery; yet the ideogram *bu* also means to cease the struggle. In Budo the point is not only to compete, but to find peace and mastery of the self.

Do, the way, is the method, the teaching that enables you to understand perfectly the nature of your own mind and self. It is the way of the Buddha, *butsudo,* that leads you to discover your own original nature, to awaken from the numbness of the sleeping ego (the little self, the limited "me") and accede to higher, fuller personhood. In Asia this way has become the supreme morality and essence of all religions and philosophies. The yin and yang of the *I Ching,* the "existence is nothing" of Lao Tsu, have their roots in it.

What does this mean? That you can forget your personal body and mind; attain absolute spirit, nonego. Harmonize, unite sky and earth. The inner mind lets thoughts and emotions pass by; it is completely free from its environment, egoism drops away. This is the wellspring of the philosophies and religions of Asia. Mind and body, outside and inside, substance and phenomena: these pairs are neither dualistic nor opposed, but form one unseparated whole. Change, any change, influences all actions, all relationships among all existences; the satisfaction or dissatisfaction of one person influences every other person; our movements and those of others are interdependent. "Your happiness must be my happiness and if you weep I weep with you. When you are sad I must become sad and when you are happy I must be so too." Everything in the universe is connected, everything is osmosis. You cannot separate any part from the whole: interdependence rules the cosmic order.

Throughout five thousand years of the history of the East, the sages and philosophers have fixed their attention on this spirit, this way, and transmitted it.

The *Shin Jin Mei* is a very ancient book, originally Chinese, and at one point it says, *shi dobu nan*—the way, the highest way, is not difficult, but you must not make choices. You must entertain neither affection nor distaste. The *San Do Kai* (or "interpenetration of essence and phenomena") says, similarly, "If you cherish one single illusion, separation comes, as between mountain and river."

One of the things Zen means is the effort of practicing meditation, zazen. It is the effort to reach the realm of thought without discrimination, consciousness beyond all categories, embracing and transcending every conceivable expression in language. This dimension can be attained through the practice of zazen and of Bushido.

THE FLUID MIND
By D.T. Suzuki, Zen and Japanese Culture

The delusive mind may be defined as the mind intellectually and effectively burdened. It thus cannot move on from one topic to another without stopping and reflecting on itself, and this obstructs its native fluidity. The mind then coagulates before it makes a second move, because the first move still lingers there—which is a *suki* for the swordsman—the one thing that is to be avoided with the utmost scrupulosity. This corresponds to the mind conscious of itself (*ushin no shin* in Japanese). To be conscious is characteristic of the human mind as distinguished from the animal mind. But when the mind becomes conscious of its doings, it ceases to be instinctual and its commands are colored with calculations and deliberations-—which means that the connection between itself and the limbs is no longer direct because the identity of the commander and his executive agents is lost. When dualism takes place, the whole personality never comes out as it is in itself. Takuan calls this situation "stopping," "halting," or "freezing." One cannot bathe in solid ice, he would warn us. Consciousness and its consequent dichotomy bring rigidity to the freely-flowing original mind, and the delusive mind begins functioning—which is fatal to the life of the swordsman.

The conscious mind is *ushin no shin* contrasting with *mushin no shin,* mind unconscious of itself. *Mushin* literally means "no-mind," it is the mind negating itself, letting go itself from itself, a solidly frozen mind allowing itself to relax into a state of perfect unguardedness.

THE MIND OF NO-MIND
By D.T. Suzuki, Zen and Japanese Culture

A M I N D unconscious of itself is a mind that is not at all disturbed by affect of any kind. It is the original mind and not the delusive one that is chock-full of affects. It is always flowing, it never halts, nor does it turn into a solid. As it has no discrimination to make, no affective preference to follow, it fills the whole body, pervading every part of the body, and nowhere standing still. It is never like a stone or a piece of wood. [It feels, it moves, it is never at rest.] If it should find a resting place anywhere, it is not a mind of no-mind. A no-mind keeps nothing in it. It is also called *munen,* "no-thought." *Mushin* and *munen* are synonymous.

When *mushin* or *munen* is attained, the mind moves from one object to another, flowing like a stream of water, filling every possible corner. For this reason the mind fulfills every function required of it. But when the flowing is stopped at one point, all the other points will get nothing of it, and the result will be a general stiffness and obduracy. The wheel revolves when it is not too tightly attached to the axle. When it is too tight, it will never move on. If the mind has something in it, it stops functioning, it cannot hear, it cannot see, even when a sound enters the ears or a light flashes before the eyes. To have something in mind means that it is preoccupied and has no time for anything else. But to attempt to remove the thought already in it is to refill it with another something. The task is endless. It is best, therefore, not to harbor anything in the mind from the start. This may be difficult, but when you go on exercising *kufu* toward the subject, you will after some time come to find this state of mind actualized without noticing each step of progress. Nothing, however, can be accomplished hurriedly.

ZAZEN

Three Essentials of Sitting

I. Disposition of the body: Full lotus, half lotus, or Japanese-style postures

A. Spine erect
B. Chin in
C. Teeth together
D. Lower eyes 45 degrees but not closed
E. Tongue to upper palate
F. Hands form a cup with both thumbs touching

II. Disposition of the mind: Mind empty with no thought. If thought enters the mind, do not hold it, let it go.

III. Disposition of the breath

A. All breathing should be done through the nose.
B. First breath should be an exhalation emptying the lungs of any carbon monoxide.
C. Second breath should be deep into the *hara*.
D. Then normal breathing should follow.

Spring comes, and the grass grows by itself.

Zen saying

AN ANECDOTE ABOUT TSUKAHARA BOKUDEN
(One of the Greatest Swordsmen, 1490 – 1572)

When Bokuden was crossing Lake Biwa in a rowboat with a number of passengers, there was among them a rough-looking samurai, stalwart and arrogant in every possible way. He boasted of his skill in swordsmanship, saying that he was the foremost man in the art. The fellow passengers were eagerly listening to his blatant talk, while Bokuden was dozing as if nothing were going on about him. This irritated the braggart very much. He approached Bokuden and shook him saying, "You also carry a pair of swords, why not say a word?" Answered Bokuden quietly, "my art is different from yours; it consists not in defeating others, but in not being defeated." This incensed the fellow immensely.

"What is your school then?"

"Mine is known as the mutekatsu school" (which means to defeat the enemy "without hands," that is without using a sword).

"Why, then do you yourself carry a sword?"

"This is meant to do away with selfish motives, and not to kill others."

The man's anger now knew no bounds, and he exclaimed in a most impassioned manner, "Do you really mean to fight me with no swords?"

"Why not?" was Bokuden's answer.

The braggart samurai called out to the boatman to row toward the nearest land. But Bokuden suggested that it would be better to go to the nearest island farther off because the mainland might attract people who were liable to get hurt somehow. The samurai agreed. The boat headed toward a solitary island at some distance. As soon as they were near enough, the samurai jumped off the boat and drawing his sword was all ready for combat. Bokuden leisurely took off his own sword and handed it to the boatman. To all appearances he was about to follow the samurai onto the island, when Bokuden suddenly took the oar away from the boatman and pushing it against the land, gave a hard backstroke to the boat. Thereupon the boat made a precipitous departure from the island and plunged into the deeper water safely away from the man. Bokuden smilingly remarked, "This is my 'no-sword' school."

In D. T. Suzuki's Zen and Japanese Culture

CUTTING UP AN OX

By Chuang-Tzu

Cook Ting was cutting up an ox for Lord Wen-Hui. At every touch of his hand, every heave of his shoulder, every move of his feet, every thrust of his knee—zip! zoop! He slithered the knife along with a zing, and all was in perfect rhythm, as though he were performing the dance of the Mulberry Grove or keeping time to the Ching-shou music.

"Ah, this is marvelous!" said Lord Wen-hui. "Imagine skill reaching such heights!"

Cook Ting laid down his knife and replied, "What I care about is the Way, which goes beyond skill. When I first began cutting up oxen, all I could see was the ox itself. After three years I no longer saw the whole ox. And now—now I go at it by spirit and don't look with my eyes. Perception and understanding have come to a stop and spirit moves where it wants. I go along with the natural makeup, strike in the big hollows, guide the knife through the big openings, and follow things as they are. So I never touch the smallest ligament or tendon, much less a main joint.

"A good cook changes his knife once a year—because he cuts. A mediocre cook changes his knife once a month—because he hacks. I've had this knife of mine for nineteen years and I've cut up thousands of oxen with it, and yet the blade is as good as though it had just come from the grindstone. There are spaces between the joints, and the blade of the knife has really no thickness. If you insert what has no thickness into such spaces, then there's plenty of room—more than enough for the blade to play about in. That's why after nineteen years the blade of my knife is still as good as when it first came from the grindstone.

"However, whenever I come to a complicated place, I size up the difficulties, tell myself to watch out and be careful, keep my eyes on what I'm doing, work very slowly, and move the knife with the greatest subtlety, until—plop! the whole thing comes apart like a clod of earth crumbling to the ground. I stand there holding the knife and look all around me, completely satisfied and reluctant to move on, and then I wipe off the knife and put it away."

"Excellent!" said Lord Wen-hui. "I have heard the words of Cook Ting and learned how to care for life!"

HOW LONG MUST I STUDY?

A young boy traveled across Japan to the school of a great and famous swordsman. When he arrived at the school he was given an audience with the founder, who was impressed that this young boy had made such a long and arduous journey.

“What do you wish from me?” the master asked.

“I wish to be your student and become the finest swordsman in the land,” the boy replied. “How long must I study?”

“Ten years at least,” the master replied.

“Ten years is a long time. What if I study twice as hard as all of the other students?”

“Twenty years,” the master replied.

“Twenty years! What if I practice unrelentingly, day and night with all of my effort?”

“Thirty years,” the master replied.

“How is it that each time I say I will work harder you tell me that it will take longer?” the boy asked, quite confused by now.

“The answer is clear,” the master said. “When there is one eye fixed upon your destination, there is only one eye left to find the Way.”

THE WOODCUTTER

A woodcutter was busily engaged in cutting down trees in the remote mountains. An animal called "satori" appeared. It was a very strange-looking creature, not usually found in the villages. The woodcutter wanted to catch it alive. The animal read his mind: "You want to catch me alive, do you not?" Completely taken aback, the woodcutter did not know what to say, whereupon the animal remarked, "You are evidently astonished at my telepathic faculty." Even more surprised, the woodcutter then conceived the idea of striking it with one blow of his ax, when the satori exclaimed, "Now you want to kill me." The woodcutter felt entirely disconcerted, and fully realizing his impotence to do anything with this mysterious animal, he thought of resuming his business. The satori was not charitably disposed, for he pursued him, saying, "So at last you have abandoned me."

The woodcutter did not know what to do with this animal or with himself. Altogether resigned, he took up his ax and , paying no attention whatever to the presence of the animal, vigorously and singlemindedly resumed cutting trees. While so engaged, the head of the ax flew off its handle, and struck the animal dead.

In D.T. Suzuki's <u>Zen and Japanese Culture</u>

THE SWORDSMAN AND THE CAT

There was once a swordsman called Shoken, who was very much annoyed by a furious rat in his house. The rat was bold enough to come out of its hiding place even in the daytime, doing all kinds of mischief. Shoken made his pet cat go after it, but she was not its equal, and being bitten by it, she ran away screaming. The swordsman now hired some of the neighboring cats noted for their skill and courage in catching rats. They were let loose against the rat. Crouching in a corner, it watched the cats approach it and furiously attacked them one after another. The cats were terrified and all beat a retreat.

The master became desperate and tried to kill the rat himself. Taking up his wooden sword he approached it, but every effort of the experienced swordsman proved ineffectual, for the rat dodged his sword so skillfully that it seemed to be flying through the air like a bird or even lightning. Before Shoken could follow its movement, it had already made a successful leap at his head. He was perspiring heavily and finally decided to give up the chase.

As a last resort, he sent for the neighboring Cat widely known for her mysterious virtue as the most able rat-catcher. The Cat did not look in any way especially different from other cats that had been invited to fight the rat. The swordsman did not think very much of her, but let her go into the room where the rat was located. The Cat went in quietly and slowly as if she were not cognizant of any unusual scene in the room. The rat, however, was extremely terrified at the sight of the approaching object and stayed motionless, almost stupefied, in the corner. The Cat almost nonchalantly went for the rat and came out carrying it by the neck.

In the evening, all the cats who had participated in the rat-catching had a grand session at Shoken's house, and respectfully asked the great Cat to take the seat of honor. They made profound bows before her and said: "We are all noted for valor and cunning, but never realized that there was such an extraordinary rat in the world. None of us was able to do anything with it until you came; and how easily you carried the day! We all wish you to divulge your secrets for our benefit, but before that let us see how much we all know about the art of fighting rats."

The black cat came forward and said: "I was born in a family reputed for its skill in the art. Since my kitten days I have trained myself with a view to becoming a great rat-catcher. I am able to leap over a screen as high as seven feet; I know how to squeeze myself through a tiny hole which allows a rat only. I am proficient in performing all kinds of acrobatics. I am also clever at making the rats think that I am sound asleep, but I know how to strike at them as soon as they come within my reach. Even those running over the beam cannot escape me. It is really a shame that I had to retreat before that old rat today."

The great veteran Cat said: "What you have learned is the technique of the art. Your mind is ever conscious of planning how to combat the opponent. The reason why the ancient masters devised the technique is to acquaint us with the proper method of accomplishing the work, and the method is naturally simple and effective, implying all the essential points of the art. Those who follow the master fail to grasp his principle and are too busily occupied with improving their technical cleverness and manipulatory skill. The end is achieved, and cleverness attains its highest efficiency, but what does it all amount to? Cleverness is an activity of the mind, no doubt, but it must be in accordance with the Way. When the latter is neglected and mere cleverness is aimed at, it diverges and is apt to be abused. This is to be remembered well in the art of fighting."

The tiger cat now stepped forward and expressed his view thus" "To my mind, what is important in the art of fighting is the spirit (*ki*; *ch'i* in Chinese); I have long trained myself in its cultivation and development. I am now in possession of the strongest spirit, which fills up heaven and earth. When I face an opponent, my overawing spirit is already on him, and victory is on my side even prior to actual combat. I have no conscious scheme as to the use of technical skill, but it comes out spontaneously according to change of situation. If a rat should be running over a beam, I would just gaze at him intensely with all my spiritual strength, and he is sure to fall by himself from the height and be my prisoner. But that old mysterious rat moved along without leaving any shadow. The reason is beyond me."

The grand old Cat's reply was this: "You know how to make the most of your psychic powers, but the very fact of your being conscious of it works against you; your strong psyche stands opposed to the opponent's, and you can never be sure of yours being stronger than his, for there is always a possibility of its being surpassed. You may feel as if your active vigorous psyche were filling the universe, but it is not the spirit itself, it is no more than its shadowy image. It may resemble Mencius' *Kozen no ki* (*hao-jan chi ch'i*), but in reality it is not. Mencius' *ch'i* ("spirit"), as we know, is bright and illuminating, and for this reason full of vigor, whereas yours gains vigor owing to conditions. Because of this difference in origin, there is a difference in its operation. The one is a great river incessantly flowing, and the other is a temporary flood after a heavy rainfall, soon exhausted when it encounters a mightier onrush. A desperate rat often proves stronger than an attacking cat. It has been cornered, the right is for life and death, and the desperate victim harbors no desire but to escape unhurt. Its mental attitude defies every possible danger which may come upon it. Its whole being incarnates the fighting *ch'i* ("spirit" or "psyche"), and no cats can withstand its steel-like resistance.

The gray cat now advanced quietly and said: "As you tell us, a psyche however strong is always accompanied by its shadow, and the enemy is sure to take advantage of this shadow, though it may be the faintest one. I have for a long time disciplined myself in this way: not to overawe the enemy, not to force a fight, but to assume a yielding and conciliatory attitude. When the enemy proves strong, I just look yielding and simply follow up his movements. I act like a curtain surrendering itself to the pressure of a stone thrown at it. Even a strong rat finds no means to fight me. But the one we had to deal with today has no parallel, it refused to submit to my psychical overpowering, and was not tempted by my manifestation of a yielding psyche. It was a most mysterious creature – the like of which I have never seen in my life."

The grand old Cat answered: "What you call a yielding psyche is not in harmony with Nature; it is man-made, it is a contrivance worked out in your conscious mind. When you try by means of this to crush the opponent's positive impassioned attacking psyche, he is quick enough to detect any sign of psychic wavering which may go on in your mind. The yielding psyche thus artificially evoked produces a certain degree of muddiness and obstruction in your mind, which is sure to interfere with acuteness of perception and agility of action, for then Nature feels impeded in pursuing its original and spontaneous course of movement. To make Nature display its mysterious way of achieving things is to do away with all your own thinking, contriving, and acting; let Nature have her own way, let her act as it feels in you, and there will be no shadows, no signs, no traces whereby you can be caught; you have then no foes who can successfully resist you.

"I am not, however, going to say that all the discipline you have each so far gone through has been to no purpose. After all, the Way expresses itself through its vessels. Technical contrivances hold the Reason (*ri*, *li*) in them, the spiritual power is operative in the body, and when it is in harmony with Nature, it acts in perfect accord with environmental changes. When the yielding psyche is thus upheld, it gives a stop to fighting on the physical plane of force and is able to stand even against rocks. But there is one most essential consideration which when neglected is sure to upset everything. This is; not to cherish even a speck of self-conscious thought. When this is present in your mind, all your acts become self-willed, human-designed tricks, and are not in conformity with the Way. It is then that people refuse to yield to your approach and come to set up a psyche of antagonism on their part. When you are in the state of mind known as "mindlessness" (*mushin*), you act in unison with Nature without resorting at all to artificial contrivances. The Way, however, is above all limitations, and all this talk of mine is far from being exhaustive as far as the Way is concerned.

"Some time ago there was in my neighborhood a cat who passed all her time in sleeping, showing no sign of spiritual animal power, and looking like a wooden image. People never saw her catch a single rat, but wherever she roamed about no rats ever dared to appear in her presence. I once visited her and asked for the reason. She gave no answer. I repeated my query four times, but she remained silent. It was not that she was unwilling to answer, but in truth she did not know how to answer. So we note that one who knows speaks not a word, while one who speaks knows not. That old cat was forgetful not only to herself but all things about her, she was in the highest spiritual state of purposelessness. She was the one who realized divine warriorship and killed not. I am not to be compared to her."

Continued the Cat: “Well, I am a mere cat; rats are my food, and how can I know about human affairs? But if you permit me to say something further, you must remember that swordsmanship is an art of realizing at a critical moment the Reason of life and death, it is not meant just to defeat your opponent. A samurai ought to be always mindful of this fact and discipline himself in a spiritual culture as well as in the technique of swordsmanship. First of all, therefore, he is to have an insight into the Reason of life and death, when his mind is free from thoughts of selfishness. This being attained, he cherishes no doubts, no distracting thoughts; he is not calculating, nor does he deliberate; his Spirit is even and yielding and at peace with the surroundings; he is serene and empty-minded; and thus he is able to respond freely to changes taking place from moment to moment in his environment. On the other hand, when a thought or desire is stirred in his mind, it calls up a world of form; there is ‘I,’ there is ‘not-I,’ and contradictions ensue. As long as this opposition continues, the Way finds itself restricted and blocked; its free activities become impossible. Your Spirit is already pushed into the darkness of death, altogether losing its mysterious native brightness. How can you expect in this state of mind to rise and wager your fate against the opponent? Even when you come out victorious, it is no more than accidental, and decidedly against the spirit of swordsmanship.”

"By 'purposelessness' is not meant mere absence of things where vacant nothingness prevails. The Spirit is by nature formless, and no 'object' are to be harbored in it. When anything is harbored there, your psychic energy is drawn toward it; and when your psychic energy loses its balance, its native activity becomes cramped and no more flows with the stream. Where the energy is tipped, there is too much of it in one direction, while in another there is a shortage. Where it is too much, it overflows and cannot be controlled; where there is a shortage, it is not sufficiently nourished and shrivels up. In both cases, it is unable to cope with ever-changing situations. But when there prevails a state of 'purposelessness' [which is also a state of 'mindlessness'] the Spirit harbors nothing in it, nor is it tipped in any one direction; it transcends both subject and object; it responds empty-mindedly to environmental vicissitudes and leaves no tracks. We have in the Book of Changes (I Ching): 'There is in it no thinking, no doing [or no willing], absolute quietness, and no motion; but it feels, and when it acts, it flows through any objects and events of the world.' When this is understood in connection with the art of swordsmanship, one is nearer to the Way.”

After listening intently to the wisdom of the Cat, Shoken proposed this question: “What is meant by 'There is neither the subject nor the object'?"

Replied the Cat: “Because of the self there is the foe; when there is no self there is no foe. The foe means an opposition as the male is opposed to the female and fire to water. Whatever things have form exist necessarily in opposition. When there are no signs [of thought movement] stirred in your mind, no conflicts of opposition take place there; and when there are no conflicts, one trying to get the better of the other, this is known as 'neither foe nor self'. When, further, the mind itself is forgotten together with signs [of thought movement], you enjoy a state of absolutely-doing-nothingness, you are in a state of perfectly quiet passivity, you are in harmony with the world, you are one with it. While the foe-form ceases to exist, you are not conscious of it, nor can it be said that you are altogether unconscious of it. Your mind is cleansed of all thought movements, and you act only when there is a prompting [from the Unconscious]."

"When your mind is thus in a state of absolutely-doing-nothingness, the world is identified with your self, which means that you make no choice between right and wrong, like and dislike, and are above all forms of abstraction. Such conditions as pleasure and pain, gain and loss, are creations of your own mind. The whole universe is indeed not to be sought after outside the Mind. An old poet sings: 'When there is a particle of dust in your eye, the triple world becomes a narrow path; have your mind completely free from objects – and how much this life expands!' When even a tiny particle of sand gets into the eye, we cannot keep it open; the eye may be likened to the Mind which by nature is brightly illuminating and free from objects; but as soon as an object enters there its virtue is lost. It is said again that 'when one is surrounded by an enemy – hundreds of thousands in strength – this form [known as my Self] may be crushed to pieces, but the Mind is mine with which no overwhelming army can have anything to do'. Says Confucius: 'even a plain man of the street cannot be deprived of his will'. When, however, this mind is confused, it turns to be its own enemy. This is all I can explain here, for the master's task cannot go beyond transmitting technique and illustrating the reason for it. It is yourself who realizes the truth of it. The truth is self-attained, it is transmitted from mind to mind, it is a special transmission outside the scriptural teaching. There is here no willful deviation from traditional teaching, for even the master is powerless in this respect. Nor is this confined to the study of Zen. From the mind-training initiated by the ancient sages down to various branches of art, self-realization is the keynote of them all, and it is transmitted from mind to mind – a special transmission outside the scriptural teaching. What is performed by scriptural teaching is to point out for you what you have within yourself. There is no transference of secrets from master to disciple. Teaching is not difficult, listening is not difficult either, but what is truly difficult is to become conscious of what you have in yourself and be able to use it as your own. This self-realization is known as 'seeing into one's own being', which is *satori*. *Satori* is an awakening from a dream. Awakening and self-realization and seeing into one's own being – these are synonymous."

In D.T. Suzuki's Zen and Japanese Culture

The Way

THE WAY

By D.T. Suzuki, Zen and Japanese Culture.

To be on the alert means to be deadly serious, to be deadly serious means to be sincere to oneself, and it is sincerity that finally leads one to discover the Heavenly Way. The Heavenly Way is above the self, which is *mushin*, "no-mind," or *munen*, "no-thought." When *mushin* is realized, the mind knows no obstructions, no inhibitions, and is emancipated from the thoughts of life and death, gain and loss, victory and defeat. As long as a man is possessed of the thought of defeating the enemy, his mind will be kept fully occupied with all kinds of scheming to attain this end. If, however, the enemy happens to be more proficient in technical tactics—which is very likely the case—the defeat will not be on the side of the enemy. If both are equally matched, the outcome will be mutual killing. When a scheme meets a scheme, this is an inevitable fate. Therefore, the perfect swordsman goes beyond all manner of dichotomy, and it is in this way that he is more than a mere wielder of the sword.

THE FOUR NOBLE TRUTHS *of Buddhism*

"The first noble truth is the existence of sorrow. Birth is sorrowful, growth is sorrowful, illness is sorrowful, and death is sorrowful. Sad it is to be joined with that which we do not like. Sadder still is the separation from that which we love, and painful is the craving for that which cannot be obtained."

"The second noble truth is the cause of suffering. The cause of suffering is lust. The surrounding world affects sensation and begets a craving thirst, which clamors for immediate satisfaction. The desire to live for the enjoyment of self entangles us in the net of sorrow. Pleasures are the bait and the result is pain."

"The third noble truth is the cessation of sorrow. He who conquers the self will be free from lust. He no longer craves and the flame of desire finds no material to feed upon. Thus it will be extinguished."

"The fourth noble truth is the eightfold path that leads to the cessation of sorrow. There is salvation for him whose self disappears before Trust, whose will is bent upon what he ought to do, whose sole desire is the performance of his duty. He who is wise will enter this path and make an end of sorrow."

"There is self and there is truth. Where self is, truth is not. Where truth is, self is not. Self is individual separateness and that egotism which begets envy and hatred. Self is the yearning for pleasure. There is no wrong in this world, no vice, no sin, except that flows from the assertion of self."

THE EIGHT-FOLD PATH
of Buddhism

Right Understanding: We must keep ourselves free from prejudices and delusion and strive to understand aright the true nature of life.

Right Mindedness: A realization that we have come of age spiritually and a consequent determination to put away childish things and interest ourselves in the larger issues.

Right Speech: Kind, plain and truthful words.

Right Action: Deeds that are peaceable, righteous, benevolent and pure.

Right Livelihood: To earn our living in such a way that we do no harm to any sentient being.

Right Endeavor: To direct our efforts incessantly to the overcoming of ignorance and craving desire.

Right Recollectedness: Remembering in moments of weakness all resolutions taken and all past experience.

Right Meditation: A complete withdrawal of perception from and thinking about external objects.

EXIT

FINDING A DOJO

By Wayne F. Tourda

Like so many things in life, some of the best are the most difficult to find. A dojo is no different. As nothing in nature is by accident, there is a reason why the best dojos with the best instructors are very low profile. For those of you who have been in the martial arts for some time, this appears to be quite obvious. For those of you who for the first time are just now being exposed to the martial arts, I would like to include these key characteristics in finding a credible dojo. It is hoped that some of these simple guidelines will enable you to select a good dojo more intelligently.

A. Suggestions for finding a dojo.
   1. If classes in the martial arts are offered at the college level in your area, perhaps the college is a good place to start; fees are minimal and established by the individual college, eliminating any profit motive.
      a. Find a college or university that teaches Eastern Studies and/or any of the martial arts as an *integral* part of the curriculum.
      b. This determines that the instructor has at least an M.A. degree in Physical Education, a teaching credential (if community college), is first-aid certified, and that the instructor's teaching methods are evaluated by an administrator yearly.
      c. Speak with the instructor about finding a credible dojo.
   2. If there is no college or university in your area, you can of course check the yellow pages, provided you follow the guidelines below in making your selection.

B. Visit: Call the dojo and make an appointment to interview the owner. A good dojo will allow you to watch as much and as long as you like without soliciting you.
   1. Questions to ask the owner or manager of the dojo:
      a. Whom did he (or she) study under?
      b. How long has he been studying?
      c. What is the emphasis of this school? Is it *Do* (way) or *Jitsu* (self-defense)?
      d. Does he have liability insurance? If so, who is the carrier?
   2. Things to look for:
      a. Does the dojo offer a sense of community?
      b. Is there a sense of cooperation among the students you are observing?
      c. Is the instructor talking to them or at them? Is he like the conductor of an orchestra?
      d. Does he command a sense of respect and does he inspire rigorous courtesy?
      e. Does he explain the important historical and theoretical evolution of the technique?
      f. Does he define and demonstrate the techniques in a clear and precise way?

HOW TO FIND AN AIKIDO DOJO

By Susan Perry

Aikido cannot be learned from books or from teachers who have learned from books. To study Aikido, one needs to find a qualified teacher and, probably, to join a school. And, as Aikido becomes better known, more fashionable, and more lucrative, potential students need to be increasingly careful in choosing teachers and schools.

But how should people go about choosing? When deciding whether to join a certain Aikido school, what should people think about? What should they look for in a teacher? Here are some suggestions:

Shop Around!

Since Aikido has found its way onto the silver screen, some greedy martial arts instructors have begun using the word "Aikido" very loosely. Do not let anyone convince you that Aikido and Aikijutsu are the same (a *do* is a Pathway, while a *jutsu* is a system of technique). And, don't let anyone tell you that Aikido is "just another martial art" whose technique can be mixed with those of fighting systems. According to its founder Aikido is "a divine path that leads to truth, goodness, and beauty and a spiritual path reflecting the unlimited, absolute nature of the universe" – not just a system of martial technique.

It is natural for American students to think about dojos on the model of private health clubs. "I'll pay my dues," a prospective student may think, "and I will expect to receive instruction and certain services in return." But many [of the more traditional dojos] run on a different model. In some, students are expected to take on more and more responsibility for the dojo's maintenance and instruction programs as they advance in rank. In others, members are expected to pay their dues even when they do not show up for classes. Participation in the dojo's programs may be regarded as a privilege rather than as something bought and paid for with membership dues.

After locating a school that interests you, visit it and look around.

Ask whether you can watch a class. If the instructor says "No" or asks you to pay for watching, that's a bad sign. Watching is the only way to tell what you are getting into, and most good teachers want you to do that before you sign up. A few teachers even *require* prospective students to watch a class or two before enrolling in their schools.

The *feeling* of the dojo is very important. Sit down and look around. Do you feel comfortable? Do you want to stay or to get up and leave? Are you edgy? Does the place feel hostile? In the West, we tend to dismiss considerations of these sorts, but they are probably the most important. Search for the proper feeling rather than for fancy furnishings.

Watching a class, your attention will probably go first to the teacher. But it is also important to look carefully at the students. It's important to ask yourself whether its students are people you like being around. Do you feel welcome in the dojo? Do the students smile? Do they help one another? Are they willing to talk to you? The answers to these questions can tell you a lot about a school.

Look at the students and see how many seem injured. See if there are an unusual number of braced knees, taped toes, and bound wrists. Injuries sometime occur in the finest Aikido classes, as they do in all classes involving physical activity. A few braces or bandages are to be expected. But if everyone in the room is wearing a brace of some sort and the practice seems rough, think carefully about joining the dojo. It may be that the people in the group practice recklessly.

Ask yourself whether the students in the dojo seem to be flourishing. Do the advanced students seem stable, confident, happy, and humble? Are they at least striving to develop these qualities through their training?

Be careful in choosing a teacher.

According to an old maxim, it's better to spend three years looking for the right teacher than to train for three years with the wrong teacher. But how can a student tell the right Aikido teacher from the wrong one? Judge the teachers on the basis of their students. Students tend to reflect their teachers' personalities. Brutal teachers tend to attract and keep brutal students, dedicated teachers tend to attract and keep dedicated students, and so on.

Aikido is a deep and rewarding art of self-transformation, not just a system of wrist locks and control holds. Don't cheat yourself. Find a deep teacher who embodies your aspirations, one who "walks his or her talk," one whose opinions you respect. Expect the teacher to challenge your views, to push you beyond what you perceive as your limits, to care for you, to talk to you, to advise you, and to be honest with you.

Aikido is unusual in that it has a technical side and a philosophical side which students must integrate. Some teachers pass on technique without any knowledge of the art's philosophical principles. Others talk philosophically the whole class without demonstrating or discussing Aikido's physical aspect. The best teachers are those who achieve a balance.

When signing up for an Aikido program, carefully examine the obligations that you are undertaking.

Many Aikido schools have their own handbooks, which they give out when you register. If you are given a handbook, read it carefully. Most schools will ask you to sign a liability waiver before you step on the mat. Don't let this frighten you. By asking students to sign waivers, the school is merely alerting them that the practice they are undertaking is physically demanding and potentially dangerous.

If you are asked to sign a contract, don't be impulsive. Take a copy home and read it over when you won't be distracted.

Beware of schools that *promise* rank or instructor status after a certain period of training. Don't waste your time on an instructor who trades rank or status for money!

DOJO ETIQUETTE

By Wayne F. Tourda

Dojo etiquette is a very important part of Aikido training and should be observed at all times. Japanese forms of etiquette are unfamiliar to most people, but over time, these forms will become comfortable expressions of courtesy. Furthermore, as our training continues, the meaning behind the forms is understood at an increasingly higher level.

One of the most basic forms of etiquette is the bow, a gesture of respect, gratitude, trust and humility. Upon entering the dojo, we face the front of the mat and bow. This shows respect for nature and the founder of Aikido. If we see the instructor (properly addressed as "Sensei") we greet him or her by bowing and saying "Osu," which is a Japanese greeting. Whenever we have been taught a technique or have been corrected in a technique, we bow and say either "Osu" or "Thank you."

Another way in which we show our respect for Aikido, the dojo, and the teacher, is by not shouting, cursing, or becoming angry on the mat. When you are asked a question, the proper response is "Hai!", which means "yes" or "OK."

If there is a disagreement, it is best to ask the teacher what is correct. If the teacher is off the mat, students should treat the senior student(s) (properly addressed as "Sempai") with the same respect as the teacher.

Effort should be made to be on time for class, and personal needs should be taken care of prior to class. If you are unavoidably late, perform the formal bow individually before beginning to practice. During class, if there is some emergency and you wish to stop practice or leave the mat, simply inform the instructor and do an individual bow as the close of your own practice.

For reasons of safety, respect, and courtesy, it is essential that the teacher's instructions be followed exactly. Many Aikido techniques can be dangerous if not practiced properly. Therefore, if you wish to practice something other than what you have been asked to practice, you should ask the permission of the instructor.

If at any time you become excessively tired and feel you must rest, simply bow to your partner and kneel, facing each other. When you are ready to resume practice, stand up, bow to your partner and resume. If at any time your dogi (uniform) becomes disarranged during practice, the same procedure should be followed; kneel together, fix your dogi, stand, bow to each other, and then resume practice.

Observation of these forms of etiquette will help to create a good atmosphere in the dojo. But it is not the superficial observation of a particular form of etiquette which is most important. Rather it is the sincere and open-hearted attitude toward training which ultimately gives meaning to the form.

DOJO TERMINOLOGY

AI	Harmony
AI-HANMI	Both partners using the same stance
ATEMI	Blow delivered at a vulnerable point of the body
BOKKEN	Wooden sword used in practice
BUDO	The Way of the Warrior
BUSHIDO	The Warrior's Code
DAN	Aikido rank or grade; black belt ranks
DO	Way, path, or approach
DOJO	Way-place, or training hall
GI	White training uniform
GYAKU-HANMI	Partners are in opposite stance
HAI	Yes, O.K.
HAJIME	Command to begin or start practice
HAKAMA	Wide-skirted black pants worn over the GI
IKKAJO	First control
IRIM	Entering into the line of attack
JO	Wooden staff used in practice
KAMAE	Basic stance
KI	Spirit; universal creative energy
KYU	Aikido rank or grade; white and brown belt ranks
MAAI	Proper distance between partners

NIKAJO	Second control
OSU	Positive or affirmative greeting
RANDORI	Freestyle against multiple approaches
REI	Bow
SEIZA	Formal sitting position
SEMPAI	Senior student
SENSEI	Teacher; literally, "one who has gone before"
SENSEI-NI-REI	Bow to the sensei
SHE-TE	Person receiving the attack and executing the technique
SHOMEN-NI-REI	Bow in the front
TANTO	Wooden knife used in practice
TATTE	Command to "stand up" from Seiza position
UKE	Person executing an approach or attack and being thrown
UKEMI	Breakfalls
WAZA	Technique
YAME	Command to stop; attention position
YOI	Ready
ZANSHIN	Completion of technique, maintaining awareness and stance; following through
ZA-ZEN	Sitting meditation

JAPANESE COUNTING

ICHI	One	**ROKU**	Six
NI	Two	**SHICHI**	Seven
SAN	Three	**HACHI**	Eight
SHI	Four	**KU**	Nine
GO	Five	**JU**	Ten

Introduction to

Basic Movements

BEGINNER COURSE OUTLINE FOR AIKIDO

BASIC MOVEMENTS

1. Basic Stance
2. Elbow Power #1
   Elbow Power #2
3. 95 Degree Pivot
4. Front Step-In with Cross-Step
5. Front Step-In with Shuffle
6. 180 Degree Pivot
7. 180 Degree Pivot with Cross-Step
8. After Class Exercise #1
9. After Class Exercise #2

BASIC TECHNIQUES

1. Cross hand grasp 2nd control (take down)
2. Cross hand grasp 2nd control with elbow lock
3. Front strike 1st control with elbow lock
4. Cross hand grasp 1st control. #1
5. One hand grasp side step-in throw. #1
6. Front strike 1st control. (basic. open-side)
7. Front strike elbow lock. (basic. open side)
8. Front strike elbow lock #1
9. Shoulder grasp elbow lock #2. (basic. open-side)
10. One hand grasp all-direction throw #1
11. Behind both hands grasp 2nd control. (take down)
12. One hand grasp (hitting-elbow) Breath throw. #1
13. One hand grasp (hitting-elbow) Breath throw. #2
14. One hand grasp elbow control. #1
15. Front strike elbow control. #1
16. Front strike elbow control #2
17. One hand grasp 2nd control. #1
18. Both hand grasp 2nd control. #1

Uchi-Deshi Program

UCHI-DESHI/ INSTRUCTOR PROGRAM

By Wayne F. Tourda

Since the acquisition of sixteen acres of land in Fallbrook, California, I am pleased to announce that we now have an Uchi-Deshi Program in Southern California. The uchi-deshi/instructor's program is modeled after the traditional uchi-deshi programs. *Uchi-deshi*, which means "live-in student" or "live-in apprentice," is in essence a form of apprenticeship in the martial arts in which the student lives alongside the teacher to acquire the skills necessary to become a professional instructor. The skills learned in the apprenticeship are not limited to the technical aspects of the art, but also encompass development in communication, marketing, administrative and leadership skills.

In the western world, an equivalent concept flourished for hundreds of years prior to the industrial revolution. The *guild system* was a form of "live-in apprenticeship" where promising students were apprenticed to a master craftsman in a given skill or trade. In exchange for their training students worked for their teachers, often over periods of many years, until they attained recognition as being fully skilled in their chosen field.

The uchi-deshi/instructor's program follows the same program I completed in Zen, which placed emphasis on both physical and philosophical training. I was greatly honored to have the opportunity to serve as an uchi-deshi under Dr. Soyu Matsuoka.

Applying for the uchi-deshi program is not a decision to be made lightly. In fact, it is considered the worst of all offenses to waste your teacher's time by not following through with the program, teaching, and ultimately contributing to the growth of Aikido.

Our primary concern is producing teachers who are committed to elevating Aikido in the eyes of the community at large. We are not interested in producing teachers whose main concern is increasing their personal income. The martial arts community has too many of these individuals already. Indeed, we feel that it is primarily greed that accounts for the sad state of affairs in modern martial arts schools. We also do not feel that desires for power or prestige are appropriate motives. Those applying for the uchi-deshi program are urged to evaluate their intentions before they apply, and if accepted, make sure that their motives remain pure.

Although the reason for the uchi-deshi program is in part to produce Aikido teachers, being an uchi-deshi involves much more than simply learning to be a professional. Indeed, it involves a great deal more. As many uchi-deshis before you have found, being an uchi-deshi is one of the most powerful and valuable educational experiences you can have.

REQUIREMENTS

Students may apply for the uchi-deshi/instructor's program anytime after having earned the rank of 4th Kyu (e.g., up through and beyond shodan); however, potential applicants should consider the following:

1) You must be at least 25 years old before you can begin the program.

2) There is a minimum one-year waiting period between the application date and the formal acceptance into the program. For example, if a student applies at 3rd Kyu they may be 2nd Kyu before they actually receive a letter of acceptance.

3) It is a four-year program (beginning at the earliest after having earned the rank of 3rd Kyu). This means that participants are expected to fulfill the obligations listed below for a four-year period.

4) It may take longer than four years (from formal acceptance) to obtain the rank of Shodan and/or receive your Level 6 instructors certificate [levels range from 6 (lowest) to 1 (highest)].

In addition, acceptance into the program requires a Bachelor's Degree or Bachelors Degree in progress. (In order ultimately to advance to a Level 4 instructor certification, a Master's Degree or equivalent is required.)

MANDATORY CLASS PARTICIPATION

Regularly Scheduled Sessions

Uchi-deshis must attend all evening classes (beginning, intermediate, and advanced). It is in the student's best interest to attend as many other classes as possible, e.g. the morning sessions. However, these sessions would be considered "in addition to" rather than "in lieu of" the evening classes. **Evening classes are mandatory.**

Special Sessions

Uchi-deshis must attend any and all clinics, demonstrations, and workshops held outside the dojo as well as any and all special classes or training sessions held at the dojo (e.g. kenshu, weapons classes, etc.). Exceptions may be made in cases where these events conflict with ongoing Aikido programs for which the uchi-deshi is assisting.

NOTE: Uchi-deshis will always be informed as far in advance as the situation allows. This should help uchi-deshis plan work schedules and other outside commitments.

However, you should keep in mind that participation in these classes and events should be considered the priority.

Meditation Sessions

After having earned the rank of 1st Kyu, uchi-deshis must attend **all** meditation sessions until they have obtained the rank of Shodan (this will be a minimum of one year). If formal zazen sessions are being held, uchi-deshis must also attend at least one formal zazen session during that year.

ASSISTANTSHIP AND STUDENT-TEACHING

Uchi-deshis may be required to assist in ongoing programs outside the dojo (community service programs, college curriculum classes, corporate/business classes, etc.) This may include student teaching as well as assisting.

NOTE: Optimally, uchi-deshis will not begin teaching on their own until after having earned the rank of Shodan and received their Level 6 teaching certificate. However, under certain circumstances (dictated by the demand for classes) uchi-deshis of lower rank and/or those who have not obtained their Level 6 teaching certificate may be asked to teach. In situations such as these, uchi-deshis will be classified as "student teachers" and will not receive monetary compensation. Monies earned from these classes will be donated to the dojo.

OPEN-CLASS SUPERVISION REQUIREMENTS

Uchi-deshis must preside over the Friday night open sessions for a minimum of one year (to begin, at the earliest, after having earned the rank of 2nd Kyu). Although an attempt will be made to keep this requirement to a one-year period, it may become necessary to extend the one-year time period. Uchi-deshis should be prepared for this possibility. Whether or not the one-year period will be extended will depend on the number of qualified uchi-deshis (i.e., 2nd Kyu or above) which are available to take the class. Those with Level 6 instructor's certificate and above are generally not asked to supervise the open-class.

DOJO MAINTENANCE

Uchi-deshis may be asked to arrive at the Dojo 20 minutes before the first evening class begins. This time is to be spent performing any necessary chores (e.g. light incense and candle, vacuum offices, dump trash, etc.). If these chores have been done, uchi-deshis should check to see if there is anything to be done (e.g. check for cobwebs, dusty items, unorganized cabinets, catching up on administrative tasks, etc.). The point is that uchi-deshis should not be idle. Uchi-deshis must also stay as late as necessary to complete all evening chores. These chores are carried out after the last evening class has ended. If an uchi-deshi has finished with his chores and, if another student (not an uchi-deshi) is completing a chore, the uchi-deshi should ask if he might take over so that the other student is free to leave.

Uchi-deshis may also be asked to organize and supervise biannual dojo cleanings. At minimum, uchi-deshis are expected to help with these biannual cleanings.

Miscellaneous maintenance responsibilities may include but are not limited to the following:

- Seeing that all cleaning equipment (e.g. vacuums) is in working order.
- Checking and replacing cleaning, bathroom and first aid supplies.
- Building or repairing any necessary fixtures, furniture, or decorations.

ADMINISTRATIVE TASKS

Uchi-deshis may be required to assist in the dojo administrative tasks. These tasks may include, but are not limited to the following:

- Updating the training log.
- Preparing the dojo calendar.
- Updating/copying dojo handouts.
- Preparing/copying dojo testing booklets.
- Preparing program proposals (e.g. college workshops).
- Preparing handouts for special classes (e.g. college workshops).
- Preparing handouts for college curriculum classes.
- Creating/copying flyers, advertisements, and brochures.

NOTE: In general, uchi-deshis are expected to volunteer to assist in any and all special dojo projects or to help in any way they can.

MANDATORY READINGS

A list of readings may be required. This reading list will vary from student to student and will consist of books and articles which the senior instructors feel are necessary to expand the uchi-deshi's knowledge of the martial arts in general, and Aikido in particular. The reading list may also include classic works that serve to expand the uchi-deshi's general knowledge.

INSTRUCTOR CERTIFICATION AND CRITERIA FOR ADVANCEMENT

LEVEL 6 CERTIFICATE:

1. Completion of the four-year uchi-deshi program.

2. Rank of Shodan.

3. Bachelors Degree from an accredited academic institution.

LEVEL 5 CERTIFICATE

1. At least two years must have elapsed since the receipt of Level 6 Certificate.

2. A minimum of 200 hours teaching experience (since the receipt of Level 6 Certificate).

3. Continual training.

   a. A minimum of two hours per week in regularly scheduled classes.

   This requirement is designed to assure continual advancement in technical skill (rather than in teaching skill). Training in mixed, intermediate, or advanced classes is required (<u>minimum of two hours per week</u>). You may also attend beginning classes. However, these sessions would be considered "in addition to" rather than "in lieu of" the more advanced classes. The only exception to this requirement would be that the individual's teaching schedule conflicts with <u>all</u> classes taught at the dojo.

   b. Kenshu classes (if offered).

   Exceptions to this include 1) teaching conflict 2) physical injury.

LEVEL 4 CERTIFICATE

1. At least two years must have elapsed since the receipt of Level 5 Certificate.

2. 200 hours teaching experience (since the receipt of Level 5 Certificate).

3. Continual training (same as above).

4. Masters Degree, teaching credential, or equivalent (e.g. state certification in a profession that requires a four-year degree from an accredited academic institution).

LEVEL 3 CERTIFICATE:

1. At least two years must have elapsed since the receipt of Level 4 Certificate.

2. 200 hours teaching experience (since the receipt of Level 4 Certificate).

3. Continual training (same as above).

4. Rank of Nidan.

LEVEL 2 CERTIFICATE

1. At least two years must have elapsed since the receipt of Level 3 Certificate.

2. 200 hours teaching experience (since the receipt of Level 3 Certificate).

3. Continual training (same as above).

LEVEL 1 CERTIFICATE

1. At least two years must have elapsed since the receipt of Level 2 Certificate.

2. 200 hours teaching experience (since the receipt of Level 2 Certificate).

3. Continual training (same as above).

4. Sandan Rank.

5. Ph.D. (or equivalent).

Advancements in teaching level will also entail continual improvement along the following lines. Evaluations of your development will be carried out by senior instructor(s) (Level 3 or above). Senior instructors will choose from one of two methods of evaluation: 1) a formal interview, or 2) less formal discussions carried out over time.

- Increase philosophical and/or theoretical understanding of Aikido.

  To improve your theoretical understanding, you might choose to further educate yourself in such subjects as biology, anatomy and physiology, physics, etc. To improve your philosophical understanding, you might choose to further educate yourself about other spiritual traditions (eastern and western).

- Contribute to the growth of Aikido.

  This might entail, for example, the initiation of new programs. It might also entail coming up with ideas to better educate the public at large about the nature of Aikido training. Or, it might entail further educating yourself in such fields as marketing, advertising, public relations, etc.

- Improve teaching ability and communication skills.

  This might entail, for example, furthering your knowledge of individual and group psychology, social behavior, collective behavior, formal organizations or political theory. (Particularly helpful in the area of political theory would be theories of human nature and philosophical and/or theoretical treatise on the formation of the ideal society.)

Please note: Insofar as Zen is intricately connected to the martial arts in general, it is highly recommended that instructors continue to attend zazen sessions at the dojo (formal and informal). Although time constraints may prevent an instructor from attending all sessions, everyone should do his or her best to attend as many as possible.

Aikido and Yoga

AIKIDO AND YOGA
By John Stevens

[It has been pointed out by John Stevens that of all the martial arts, Aikido has the most in common with yoga. Both are psychophysical disciplines that seek to link the practitioner to the universal and to create an environment of harmony and peace.]

Aikido is also yoga, a "yoke" that unifies, conjoins, and harnesses us to higher principles. The eight limbs of classical yoga parallel the teachings of Morihei's classical Aikido:

> *Yama*, "ethics," primary of which is *ahimsa*, "nonviolence." In Morihei's words, "Those who seek competition are making a grave mistake. To smash, injure, or destroy is the worst sin a human being can commit."
>
> *Niyama*, "discipline," in Aikido is termed *tanren* (forging): "The purpose of training is to tighten up the slack, toughen the body, and polish the spirit."
>
> *Asana*, "graceful postures." Sometimes it is helpful for trainees to think of Aikido movements not as lethal martial art techniques but as *asana*, physical postures that link the practitioner to higher truths. Like *asana*, Aikido techniques are painful and difficult in the beginning, but eventually they become easier, more stable, and agreeable. Indeed it is said in yoga that "the *asana* is perfect when the effort to attain it disappears" and "one who masters the *asana* conquers the three worlds." Morihei taught: "Functioning harmoniously together, right and left give birth to all techniques. The four limbs of the body are the four pillars of heaven."
>
> *Pranayama*, "breath control," is necessary to partake of the breath of the universe: "Breathe in and let yourself soar to the ends of the universe; breathe out and bring the cosmos back inside. Next, breathe up all the fecundity of earth. Finally, blend the breath of heaven and the breath of earth with your own, becoming the Breath of Life itself."
>
> *Pratyahara* connotes "freedom from bewilderment," a withdrawal from the distraction of the senses, a mind that is steadfast and imperturbable. Regarding this, Morihei instructed: "Do not stare into the eyes of your opponent: he may mesmerize you. Do not fix your gaze on his sword: he may intimidate you. Do not focus on your opponent at all: he may absorb your energy."
>
> *Dharana*, "fixing the mind," is also known as *ekagrata*, "keeping the one point," a well-known concept in Aikido circles: "If you are centered, you can move freely. The physical center is your belly; if your mind is set there as well, you are assured of victory in any endeavor."

Dhyana, "meditation," is a state of penetrating insight and clear vision: "Cast off limiting thoughts and return to true emptiness. Stand in the midst of the Great Void."

Samadhi, "total absorption," goes even further. In *samadhi*, the distinction between knower and known dissolves, a transfiguration that Morihei expressed as "I am the universe!" Morihei's supernatural powers originated in his all-absorbing *aiki samadhi*, and his eccentric behavior likewise was characteristic of the highest levels of yoga – a kind of divine madness that transcended time and space. "If you do not blend with the emptiness of the Pure Void, you will not find the path of *aiki*."

Morihei's teaching was summed up in the phrase *Takemusu Aiki*. *Take* stands for "valor and bravery;" it represents the irrepressible and indomitable courage to live. *Musu* typifies birth, growth accomplishment, fulfillment. It is the creative force of the cosmos, responsible for the production of all that nourishes life. *Takemusu Aiki* is code for "the boldest and most creative existence!"

Yoga

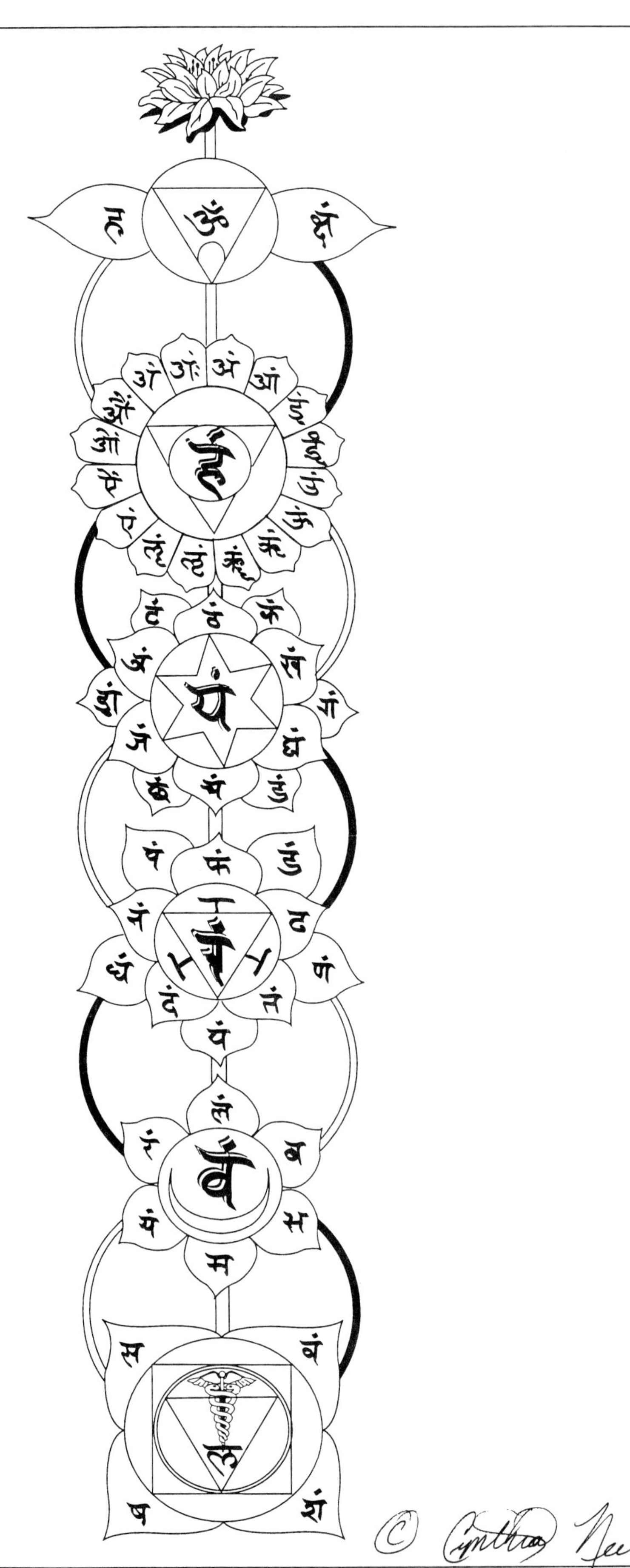
ॐ
हं
यं
वं
लं

Comments from the Yoga Faculty

COMMENTS FROM THE YOGA FACULTY

Yoga is the great mother of all mind/body arts. It is the foundation. Regardless of your practice, be it Budo, Aikido, Kendo, Kyudo, Judo or Karate-Do, practice in Yoga will deepen and enhance your understanding of the Way.

Vince McCullough (Buddhaprem)

Yoga is an inspiring and self-expressive discipline that is as relevant today as it was in its beginnings. Practicing this union of mind, body, spirit taps into our peaceful place deep inside. From that place we become renewed.

We reach our center by learning simple yoga postures, breathing techniques, and meditation exercises through which we quiet the mind.

Yoga has transformed my own life into one of greater creativity, peace, and understanding.

Claire Elkins

It has been my experience that Yoga is not about getting my students or me to "perform" physical feats of body or breath. It is my sincere desire that the practice of Yoga simply help point the way to one's true self. Yoga, which means "to join," can be a beautiful tool with which to join oneself with one's true nature. The long journey, the great search, can quite simply be found at home, literally at one with Self. A beautiful Indian story tells that a bubble searching for its true self floats along in the sea when it pops, discovering itself to be part of the ocean all along, the ocean in which it had thought itself to be separate.

The invitation is here for all of us, with vigilance and a true desire for freedom, to discover our true nature and be truly *still*.

Sharon Haas

Yoga is a personal journey. No one can do it for you. That is why it is alive, not filled with empty form and ritual. It is a 'science' that must be experienced, not theorized. It is an 'art' of discipline and observances with increasing levels of concentration and awareness. With yoga we learn to tune out outside distractions and disturbances and tune in to our own inner natures and rhythms.

To share with you the genesis of my love of yoga, let me quote one of my long time favorite friends, a book called the I Ching, or Book of Changes. The book is comprised of various hexagrams relating to the changes inherent in all living things. The hexagram that refers to the practice of yoga is *Ken*, Keeping Still. It reads,

> *Keeping still. Keeping his back still*
> *So that he no longer feels his body.*
> *He goes into his courtyard*
> *And does not see his people.*
> *No blame.*

> [The commentary reads:] True quiet means keeping still when it time to keep still, and going forward when the time has come to go forward. In this way movement and rest are in agreement with the demands of the time, and thus there is light in life.
>
> The hexagram signifies the end and beginning of all movement. The back is named because in the back are located all the nerve fibers that mediate movement. If the movement of these spinal nerves is brought to a standstill, the ego, with its restlessness, disappears as it were. When a man has thus become calm, he may turn to the outside world. He no longer sees in it the struggle and tumult of individual beings, and therefore he has that true peace of mind which is needed for understanding the great laws of the universe and for acting in harmony with them. Whoever acts from these deep levels makes no mistakes. (Wilhelm edition)

It is interesting to note that the Chinese Book of Changes has been held to be of such high antiquity that it antedates historical memory. It is also interesting to note that the eight trigrams comprising the foundation of the I Ching are found to occur in various combinations at a very early date. Of the two collections from antiquity, the first Book of Changes, belonging to the Hsia Dynasty (according to tradition 2205–1766 B.C.E.), is said to have begun with the hexagram *Ken*, Keeping Still. Which would indicate how much value the legendary sages of the Chinese culture placed on the practice of yoga!

Troyce Thome

SILENT BEGINNINGS

My mind is always churning
It doesn't stop to rest
I seek the silent spaces
To sort out what is best

Slow down and stop all actions
And listen carefully
To what the body tells me
To what I need to see

Be patient.....Trust the process
Give permission to be free
Of doubts and fears that plague me
And stop me being me

LET GO OF PAST AND FUTURE
In the hour I am here
Stay in the present moment
Release...Renew...Get clear

Give honor to the wisdom
That comes each time I breathe
Beyond all thoughts and thinking
The gift of health received

Nancy Bessette 1/96

What is Yoga

THE MEANING OF YOGA

By Haridas Chaudhuri

Yoga is a pivotal concept in Indian culture. It has been at the source of all significant religious and philosophical movements.

Philosophic thinking in India has been concerned from the very beginning with the root crisis of the spirit in man. The basic issue of human suffering including moral, religious and psychological problems has been traced to one ultimate cause, to wit, self-estrangement, alienation from existence, loss of contact with Being. Emotional conflicts, social discords, political wars--all these, in final analysis, flow from man's loss of contact with the ground of existence (*atman* or *Brahman*). Alienation from existence makes him outwardly oriented to the point of restlessness. He eagerly looks for his happiness in the outside world. He fiercely fights for the blessings of life with rival contestants. He desperately searches for truth as an object of contemplation, as a thing to think about. He seriously endeavors to settle his accounts with fellow beings by means of objectivized principles, pacts and agreements. *He forgets that the crux of his crisis lies within himself, in the buried discrepancies of his own nature* [our italics]. Yoga calls attention to this crucial fact. It aims at that vital existential experience which reunites man with the inmost centre of his own being

THE ESSENCE OF YOGA

What then is the essence of yoga? The word yoga is derived from the Sanskrit root-verb *yuj* meaning bind, join, unite, control. It is allied to the English word *yoke*, the German *joch,* and the Latin *jungo* (I join). Yoga thus literally means union and control. It signifies the union of man with God, of the individual with the universal reality, of each with the All of existence. It means union of the mortal with the eternal. It implies union of the mind with the inmost center of one's own being, the self or *atman*--union of the conscious mind with the deeper levels of the unconscious--resulting in the integration of the personality. That is indeed the chief objective of yoga. But yoga also means control, that is to say, appropriate self-discipline. It is the mobilization of the inner resources of personality with a view to attaining that self-integration which religion calls God-realization, and mysticism calls immediate union with the infinite. In this sense yoga is the method or technique, the programme of psycho-physical, moral and spiritual training, by following which one can fulfill the ultimate destiny of life. The word yoga thus implies both the goal of life and the path leading to that goal. A Yogi is one who follows the spiritual path of self-discipline, or who has attained the goal of self-realization.

A basic idea in yoga is that of freedom in spiritual self-expression. Yoga does not believe in any standardized path, for all to follow. It does not stand for any rigidly fixed rule, to which all should conform. It does not offer any patent remedy for human salvation. It affirms the oneness of truth, but rejects the uniformity of living. The fundamental conviction in yoga is that there are different psychological types to which people belong. There are introverts and extroverts; there are contemplatives and activists; there are the self-analytical and impulsive, emotional and intuitive types of people. It is therefore in the fitness of things that corresponding to these different psychological types there should be different lines of self-development, or different avenues of approach to creative self-expression. *The important thing is that every individual should have the opportunity of growing from the roots of his own being, following the bent of his own nature, along the lines indicated by his own physical make-up, towards the full flowering of his individuality as a unique creative center of the cosmic whole* [our italics].

YOGA AND RELIGION

Yoga calls attention to the spiritual oneness of all mankind. Persons belonging to different religious faiths may profitably practice yoga without abandoning their particular religious affiliations and without having to undergo any new kind of religious baptism or credal conversion. For the practice of yoga it is not even necessary that a person must have faith in God, let alone any determinate conception of God. Even a skeptic or atheist may with profit practice yoga, provided only that he has a sincere desire to know the truth and a readiness to live up to his version of the truth. The basic requirement of yoga practice is the sincerity of purpose and a resolute will to carry an open-minded investigation in the realm of the spirit.

If a person starts with some kind of religious faith, yoga aims at turning that faith into a personal realization of the truth. *Yoga is not a matter of belief; it is that inner growth of consciousness which results in direct insight into the heart of reality* [our italics]. It is not conformity to scriptural injunctions or some fixed socio-cultural pattern, but progressive realization of the full freedom of the inner spirit. It endeavors to turn doubt into critical self-inquiry and faith into living experience.

One may also define yoga as a kind of universal spirituality beyond all religions. It is a non-religious spiritual orientation. It believes that when a Hindu achieves the ultimate objective of his spiritual effort, namely, integration with truth, he ceases to be a mere Hindu. Born as a Hindu he becomes a world citizen or cosmic man. When he reaches the goal of Hinduism he sees that this is also the ultimate goal of other great religions. Hinduism is thus fulfilled in his life beyond itself. Similarly, when a Christian reaches the ultimate goal of his sincere spiritual effort he ceases to be a mere Christian. Human labels cannot restrict him anymore. He becomes a cosmic man. The same is true for a sincere Buddhist, a sincere Muslim, etc. Different religions are like so many boats helping different peoples to cross the river of ignorance and self-alienation. When the other shore is reached, the boats are left behind. The content of wisdom for which the other shore stands is found to be identical. It is this concept of the identical spiritual destiny of man--this ideal of cosmic integration with the ground of existence--which is the basis of yoga.

HATHA YOGA

Hathayoga is the system which starts with the body. Body and mind being closely interrelated, it aims at mastery over the body with a view to securing corresponding mastery over the mind. Control of nervous and vital energies produces control of mental functions. The mind-body complex being brought under perfect control, the indwelling spirit shines out and the higher self is realized.

Hatha is derived from the roots, *ha* (sun) and *tha* (moon). *Hatha* is the equalization and stabilization of the 'sun breath' (i.e. the breath which flows through the right nostril) and the 'moon breath' (i.e. the breath which flows through the left nostril). *Hatha* also means violence, force. Through the regulation of the physiological processes, *Hathayoga* forcibly releases the dormant energies of human personality.

The principal steps of *Hathayoga* are *asana* and *pranayama*. *Asana* consists of certain bodily postures such as lotus posture, hero posture, head stand, shoulder stand, etc. They are designed to stimulate the glands, vitalize the body, and strengthen the nervous system. Purified and strengthened nerves are the most important pre-requisite of yogic practice

Pranayama means control of the vital energy through breath regulation. It aims at mastery over the vital forces which are operative in the body. Through control of breath and mobilization of vital forces, it endeavors to secure the release and free flow of the fundamental psycho-physical energy (*kundalini*) latent in the human system. This root energy being dynamized, the individual is set on the path leading to his reintegration with the ultimate ground of existence.

It is believed that one who acquires success in *Hathayoga* gains supernormal powers. He enjoys vibrant health, youthfulness and longevity. He attains spiritual liberation and supernal bliss.

The chief merit of *Hathayoga* lies in its insistence upon the basic importance of the body. Various bodily postures and breathing exercises recommended in *Hathayoga* are very effective means of developing the body as a fit and strong instrument of higher spiritual living. Mystics who have neglected the bodily factor, have suffered immensely on the physical plane. They have suffered from disease and disability, and have met with premature death. Profound spiritual experiences put an inordinate strain on the nervous system. They often come with the impact of a rushing flood. Without a prior bodily training and nervous firmness, many mystics fail to stand that impact. They are carried off by waves of emotion; they sing, dance, cry, and roll on the floor, failing to convert the flood of emotion into calm creative energy. *Hathayoga* can prepare and fortify one against this kind of mishap.

The chief defect of *Hathayoga* lies in its over-emphasis upon the physical side of existence. The body is sometimes almost deified. Preoccupation with the body produces excessive self-concern. Acquisition of supernormal powers and the bliss of personal salvation loom large on the mental horizon. An indifference to the affairs of the world and the requirements of society is generated. Not much interest is left for higher cultural pursuits. The need for intellectual development is not sufficiently recognized. The danger of going astray through selfish appropriation of whatever unusual power is gained is rampant. The spectacle of *Hathayogis* making a vain-glorious display in public of their extraordinary bodily control is not an uncommon sight. It is such misguided persons who have brought much disrepute upon the fair name of yoga.

PSYCHIC INTEGRATION

Psychic integration implies the harmonious growth of personality. In the interest of balanced growth, one has to come to terms with the fundamental instinctual urges of one's nature. One has to pay attention to the distinctive bent and inclination of the individual psyche. In an attempt to reconcile impulse and reason, the unconscious id and the conscious ego, one discovers a deeper principle of unity in one's existence. It is the principle of the higher self. It does not allow the lopsided development of mind at the cost of body, or of brawn at the cost of brains. It does not encourage the one-sided growth of intellect at the cost of emotion, or of sentimentalism at the sacrifice of calm judgment. It does not permit the tyrannical growth of social consciousness at the sacrifice of psychic needs or the rebellious spirit of whimsical and arbitrary behavior such as is subversive to the social order. [Yoga helps to find the balance in the apparent dichotomy of life.]

THE HISTORY OF YOGA

By Troyce Thome

The beginnings of yoga are as mystical as yoga itself. It is said to have been handed down from enlightened beings to help the mortal mind find its way back to universal consciousness or Brahman.

Traces of yoga are found in archeological digs of the ancient Indus Valley. Some of these artifacts date back to the third millenium B.C.E. or around 5,000 years ago. The archeological remains tell us much about the cultures of the earlier civilizations of Northern India. From the designs in the seals we can conclude that the yogis depicted in the seals were held in high esteem. The yogis and other wandering rishis were free and independent thinkers, often well respected by the rulers and the common people for living outside the framework of the established religion of the time.

At the time of the early civilizations in the Indus Valley from which the yoga artifacts were found, the established religion was Brahminism. This civilization had a strict caste system; the priests were all powerful, followed by the rulers. The spiritual literature of the era were the Vedas, and the era thus the era has come to be known as the Vedic era. The Brahmin priests carefully guarded the knowledge contained in the Vedas and used it to gain control over their communities. The rulers and the common people believed there were special powers in the ancient hymns, prayers and rituals conducted by the Brahmin priests.

Rare individuals who looked at the rituals as a lot of hocus pocus needed to retreat to the forest to avoid being persecuted. In time these free thinkers and wandering rishis established small groups of students of like mind whose teaching and speculations lay the foundations of modern day yoga. Its main writings were the Upanishads, which were later added to the Vedas.

Although yoga is not a religion in itself it is found at the heart of several of the older religions: Hinduism, Jainism, Buddhism and Taoism. Some of the earlier religions have all but faded away or gone through major transformations, but yoga tends to survive from the most ancient of times to modern day. Vivian Worthington states in her book A History of Yoga:

> " The reason why yoga survives, and will continue to live, is that it is a repository for something basic in the human soul and psyche. While the more esoteric forms of religion may flourish for a time, along with priesthood, caste, sacrifice, repression, conspicuous wealth, and extravagant art, buildings, elaborate theologies or complex ritual, these will all eventually expend themselves, and a particular religion either purifies itself or is taken over by something else. We can see this in the rise and decline of many of the sects of Hinduism and Buddhism, in China, Japan and Tibet. At such times the yoga stream is turned to with relief,

and a new sect will arise embodying many of its features. It has always acted from one point of view as a kind of perennial philosophy.

What are the features that people turn to at such times? They are mysticism, the idea of personal effort and discipline including self improvement, simplicity and austerity, the idea of meeting yourself and reality through meditation. . . . In the main yoga invites us to be self-reliant. . . . We no longer look to exterior forms or to another person to help us. We look to ourselves, and in yoga we find techniques and teachings ready to help us."

THE FOUR YOGAS
by Ganga White

It usually isn't long after one begins study of Yoga that a myriad of forms of Yoga are encountered. A few of the types are Hatha, Jnana, Bhakti, Karma, Kundalini, Kriya, Atma, Agni, Buddhi, Parama, Tantra, Laya and Mantra Yogas. This can all be quite confusing. The word Yoga means union, to unite or make whole. How has this science of re-integration itself become divided into so many seemingly conflicting parts? In order to understand this we must first look at a few of the major systems.

Though there are many different systems or names of Yoga systems, many scholars agree that there are four or five major types of Yoga. These are often referred to as *The Four Yogas*. . . .

RAJA YOGA. Raja means king and Raja Yoga is known as the kingly Yoga. This Yoga is usually attributed to Patanjali, who first codified this system, although he didn't call it Raja but simply a vision of Yoga. . . .

One of the appealing things about Raja Yoga is also its very limitation. It appears to be a scientific, step-by-step path to truth or enlightenment. This makes it especially attractive to the western mind, which seeks order and explanation for everything. It is the Yoga of control and what is more controlling than a king? Most interpretations of Raja Yoga emphasize controlling the mind, the senses, the life force, thought, breath and most other aspects of life. Hence when imbalanced, it can become rigid and mechanical.

BHAKTI YOGA is the Yoga of devotion. It is the most like world religions in that it consists of prayer, singing, devotional practices, study of scriptures, remembrance of God, service and rituals. Bhakti Yoga is based on cultivating faith and its goal is total self-surrender to God. It acknowledges that our own mind and understanding are quite limited and therefore it behooves us to attune to and serve God or, for the less theistic person, the higher intelligence in the universe. Bhakti Yoga seeks to lead one to the bliss and ecstasy of oneness with God. It is the path of the heart but followed blindly or to extremes can lead to the ignorance of ritualism, emotionalism and mindlessness.

JNANA YOGA is the Yoga of wisdom. It is based on the study of oneself. Jnana Yoga suggests that the supreme in life, such as divine love, truth, or God-consciousness, cannot be cultivated. These non-things cannot be brought about by our little minds and actions. Rather they come into being when we remove the obstruction of our ignorance and illusions. In its purest, non-dualist form Jnana even denies that we are ever separate from God. It says that acts of worship or seeking of God in fact deny the oneness that already exists! A famous great Jnana Yoga saying is *Tat Twam Asi* or *Thou Art That*. This not only asserts oneness but carefully uses the word *that*, which points to truth instead of naming or defining it. Rather than being based on faith, Jnana Yoga encourages inquiry and questioning. It is the Yoga of Seeing and Being, asking us to look and discover rather than to follow and believe.

Jnana Yoga has been called the *pathless path.* It endeavors to free one from conditioning and the limitations of knowledge. It shows us that when we open our eyes and begin to see the beauty and sacredness around us we do not need techniques, rituals, or beliefs. We need to end our illusion and delusion. This happens through the awakening of perception and watchfulness in our daily life. But imbalanced, Jnana can lead to intellectualism and dry, mental self-indulgence.

KARMA YOGA is the Yoga of action. We must act in the world and this Yoga seeks to bring awareness to our actions. It deals with both the quality and the motivation of action and might be called the *Yoga of doing*. We can learn to act with more clarity, completeness, beauty and meditation in action. Our businesses, our bodies, our relationships and even how we do the dishes, with right understanding, all become an expression of our Yoga. Our actions are the manifestation of our inner reality. As has been said, we can talk the talk but do we walk the walk?

Karma Yoga is the place where all Yoga systems can come together. No matter what one's point of view, when spiritual awareness awakens and the heart opens with love and compassion, its expression is in sharing with others. A danger of Yoga, and of life itself, is self-centeredness. Most Yoga practices deal with improving our minds, bodies and hearts. So we must be vigilant about becoming preoccupied with ourselves. Yoga is something far deeper than developing the body beautiful or increasing one's bliss. Karma Yoga reminds us to think of and serve others, especially those who cannot help themselves—the very poor, sick, or old. It asserts that "you are the world."

To our unawakened eyes these systems may seem to contradict each other. Bhakti says have faith, Jnana says question everything. Raja says control your mind, Jnana says the controller is that which you are trying to control! But the problem is the medium, not the message. The limitation of the very structure of mind, thought and language creates the division. When you explain that which can never be put into words, the closest you can get is paradox!

Perhaps the metaphor of a sage will help. He likened the four yogas to a bird. Raja Yoga is the tail, steering, steadying and guiding the bird with control. Bhakti and Karma, love-devotion and action are the wings propelling it onward. Jnana is the head, seeing and guiding the bird toward the light. Which part can you deny? Which can you deny and still fly?

To return to our question, what has created all this division in the science of oneness? Perhaps it is our very chattering mind. The first statement in the Tao te Ching says, *The Tao that is explained is not the Tao*. And, as ancient yogis have said, *To define Truth is to deny it*. These great sayings point out that we must become aware of the limitation of words. As soon as you explain oneness your words become a viewpoint, one perspective, and not the whole.

In doing the headstand Hatha Yogis learn to see things from a different perspective. Perhaps an upside down way of looking at the unity in Yoga could be that all paths are one because no path alone leads to truth. Therefore it is not a question of finding the right system or even the best one. What is important is realizing that no explanation or system can contain the wholeness of life.

White Lotus Foundation
2500 San Marcos Pass
Santa Barbara, CA 93105

BASIC CONCEPTS OF YOGA: ENERGY FIELDS, CHAKRAS, AND THE MIND/BODY CONNECTION

By Virginia MacIvor Meyn

Practicing Yoga is not merely a matter of putting your body through a sequence of breathing exercises and postures. It is a "matter" of aligning and balancing *energies*. Balance and harmony do not begin in the body. They begin quite literally in the energy field that surrounds your body. Quantum physics has taught us that *everything* is energy.

Electromagnetic "fields of life" emanate from all matter. Each of us radiates energy. These electromagnetic fields have been actually measured by modern scientific instruments, documented in the pioneer work of Drs. Burr and Northrop at Yale in 1935 and the more current research of New York orthopedic surgeon Robert O. Becker and his colleagues, among others.

The human field or aura is actually made up of *interpenetrating layers* of energy. Closest to and immediately surrounding the physical body is the so-called "etheric body," a vital bioenergetic field that extends about 2 to 6 inches from the surface of the skin. The aura can extend as far as several feet beyond the etheric body into increasingly subtle ranges of emotional, mental, and spiritual energy.

Our etheric body acts as a sheath that envelopes, molds, and powers our physical body. It is referred to as the vital body because it is infused by a continuously flowing, primal universal force known as *prana, chi* or *ki* that we receive from the sun, from the etheric substance of the food we eat and the water we drink, and most importantly from the air we breathe. The etheric body is a vital body because it literally holds us together and keeps us alive and well.

Connecting this etheric or pranic body to the subtler emotional, mental, and spiritual layers of energy are seven spinning force centers or vortices called *chakras*, a Sanskrit word for "wheels of light." These seven major centers or chakras are located along a vertical axis in the etheric body that corresponds to the physical spine (see illustration). Each chakram is directly linked to an endocrine gland and acts as a transformer and transmitter of the energies to that gland and into the physical region controlled by that gland. Thus the physical body is intimately affected by what we think and what we feel. *'Energy follows thought'*. This is indeed largely where disharmony begins. Attitude is everything!

So is breathing. The most important source of vital prana is the atmosphere. When we are in tune and breathe correctly, prana flows harmoniously around and through the etheric sheath, entering via the spleen chakram (a subsidiary center); we experience health and well-being. When we are out of sorts, and our breathing is not regulated, the chakras are thrown out of balance and the pathways of pranic flow become blocked and distorted. The corresponding parts of our physical bodies suffer the ill effects.

Recognition of the "fields of life" and their role in linking the physical and the mental has its roots in very early times. An example is found in a passage from the Upanishads (1200 to 800 B.C.E.). There one is urged to realize that the "body is spirit, whose form is light, whose thoughts are true, whose nature is like ether, omnipresent and invisible, from whom all works, all desires, all sweet odours and tastes proceed." Herein lies the metaphysical foundation for Yoga.

Yoga, meaning 'to unite or make whole', offers a means of re-balancing the crucial energy centers that connect mind and body. The Eight Limbs of Yoga show us the way. From these precepts we learn that Yoga postures or *asanas* are not merely mechanical gestures when proper attitude, proper living, breath-control or *pranayama*, one-pointedness of mind, and meditation are an integral part of one's program.

Sources: Bruyere's Wheels of Light; Burr's The Fields of Life; Hopking's Practical Guide to Esoteric Healing; Leadbeater's The Chakras; MacIvor and LaForest's Vibrations: Healing Through Color, Homeopathy, and Radionics; Russell's Design for Destiny; van Lysebeth's Pranayama.

Special thanks to our assistant Rochelle Higgs and my friend Barrie Jaeger for their bright and probing questions!

THE EIGHT LIMBS OF YOGA

No study of yoga would be complete without an understanding of the Eight Limbs of Yoga. The Eight Limbs of Yoga was compiled by the Sage Patanjali in the Yoga Sutras, somewhere between the 4th century B.C.E. and the 4th century C.E. They have had a most profound effect on the development and practice of yoga ever since. They are inspiring, penetrating and concise, including in their small compass all the main practices of yoga. Like so much Indian teaching these instructions are not a fully worked out system, but rather hints and suggestions.

Patanjali's yoga is really Raja Yoga, the yoga of mental processes, of mind and will power. The Sutras are a very concise and expert analysis of the human mind, its nature and functions. Patanjali's work deals with the simplest efforts at mental discipline, in a progressive series of steps or disciplines which purify the body and mind, ultimately leading the practitioner to enlightenment or samadhi.

Source: Worthington's A History of Yoga

The Eight Limbs of Yoga are:

I.	YAMA	Abstinence or following universal laws
II.	NIYAMA	Observance of proper living habits
III.	ASANA	Physical postures leading to body control
IV.	PRANAYAMA	Breath-control or control of Prana
V.	PRATYAHARA	Withdrawal of the senses or emancipation of mind
VI.	DHARANA	Concentration or one-pointedness of mind
VII.	DHYANA	Meditation or continued holding of one-pointedness
VIII.	SAMADHI	Contemplation or the state of super-consciousness

YAMAS

Yama means "restraint." Study and practice of the yama and niyamas are the extra effort sincere yoga students make to become more conscious of their motives, feelings, and actions. Study and practice of the yamas and niyamas help to deepen the experience of self-awareness beyond the level of normal consciousness. Through deepening the level of awareness we tend to overcome some of the impediments to our spiritual growth.

*Ahimsa - nonviolence, refraining from harmful thoughts and actions

*Satya - truthfulness, refraining from lying, exaggeration and pretense.

*Asteya - not stealing, refraining from taking things that don't belong to you

*Bramacharya - moderation in all things

*Aparigraha - nonpossessiveness, the practice of detachment

NIYAMAS

Niyama means "observance" (literally, "nonrestraint"). These are qualities that you practice to protect and strengthen yourself, build your concentration and reinforce your desire to learn.

*Saucha - purity, tuning up the body through right food, exercise, rest, and cleanliness.

*Santosh - contentment, being happy with where you are and having a clear idea of where you are going.

*Tapas - discipline, self-control as a necessity for spiritual growth.

*Svadhyaya - study, reading and reflection, applying the concepts to your life.

*Ishwara-Pranidhana - remembrance, recognizing the nondying part of yourself.

There is an old Buddhist saying, "As a man thinketh so he becomes." Integrate the yamas and niyamas into your daily life and watch the transformation begin.

Pranayama

WHY STUDY PRANAYAMA?

By Troyce Thome

The human mind is by nature unsteady, affected by everything around it. Sights, sounds, scents, feelings, all play a constant role in shaping the way we think and behave. Until we can find a way to still the mind amid the ceaseless input of the stimuli around us, we will forever be slaves to our external environment, living our lives as puppets on a string, victims of our own creations!

How can we begin to still the mind and free ourselves from our self-induced "whiplash"? Yogis have taught for thousands of years the "secrets" of becoming free from the machinations of our minds. The study of Raja Yoga (the science of mental control) is a combination of yogas--Mantra Yoga, Kundalini Yoga, and Hatha Yoga--designed to bring the mental processes under control. Hatha Yoga, a form of yoga that gives attention to the physical body, uses asanas and pranayama to bring the body and mind into harmony with one another. While the asanas are meditative postures for body control, pranayama is the science of controlling prana. Prana is *universal life force,* ayama means *to curb or master.* So one of the methods used by yogis to bring vital energies and emotions under control is the use of Pranayama.

> "The first aim of yoga is the control of vital energies or prana. To this end we must first establish control by our mental consciousness of all our vital and emotional reactions. This absorption by the conscious self of inframental energies gives us the strength which enables the conscious self to penetrate the regions of supramental conscience…
>
> The name Hatha Yoga has been given to the practices and disciplines which enable us to control our bodies and energies. Though this is only one of the means of yoga, it is the first preparation on the road to reintegration, the necessary starting point for a further realisation."
> (Alain Danielou, Methode de reintegration, quoted by van Lysebeth.)

Since prana is the energy or force that animates matter, it never grows less or more, but is always in constant supply, connecting all life together by a vibrating gossamer web of energy. The objective of pranayama is to tap into this source of universal energy, absorb it, store it, control it, direct it and use it for spiritual enlightenment and healing.

Mind and prana are interdependent; each one is incapable of acting independently of the other. (Observe what happens to your breath when you become extremely angry or sad.) We study pranayama to gain control over our mental chatter and over our involuntary nervous system by bringing both to vibrate in a rhythm of harmony with the universal life flow. As we train our minds to regulate, channel, and store prana, we become able to go more deeply into consciousness and to act from these levels.

The great Sage Vasishta describes the connection between mind and prana as follows, according to Swami Vishnudevananda in The Complete Illustrated Book of Yoga:

> "O Rama! For the motion of the chariot, which is the physical body, the God has created the mind and prana without which the body cannot function. When the prana departs, the mechanism of the body ceases and when the mind works prana or vital breath moves. The relation between the mind and prana is like that between the driver and the chariot. Both exert motion one upon the other. Therefore, the wise should study regulation of prana or vital breath if they desire to suspend the restless activity of the mind and concentrate. The regulation of breath brings all happiness, material and spiritual, from the acquisition of Kingdoms to Supreme Bliss. Therefore, O Rama! Study the Science of Breath!"

PRANAYAMA: BREATHING EXERCISES

By Vincent D. McCullough

The word prana signifies primal energy, and all forms of energy are derived from prana. Pranayama means control of prana and is a way of exercising so that you reduce the external breathing through the lungs while transferring the function of breathing to the internal metabolism.

Breathing has four phases:
1. Inspiration (Puraka)
2. Internal holding of breath (Khumbaka)
3. Expiration (Rechaka)
4. External holding of breath

External and internal breath are the two main classes.

External breathing consists of:
1. Ventilation, including air coming in and going out through the air passage.
2. Gaseous exchange taking place in the lungs. Apana, waste produced and carbon dioxide is removed from the blood into the air chamber. Prana, oxygen and all other parts of atmospheric air is absorbed into the blood from the air chamber of the lungs.
3. Pumping of the heart sends this oxygenated blood to every part of the body and to each cell for internal breathing.

Internal breathing is tissue and cell breathing. It is real breath in which innumerable chemical, biochemical, and biological processes are involved:
1. Oxidation and other metabolic processes.
2. Production of carbon dioxide, apana, and other waste products.

The term for breathing exercises is Pranayama. By means of breathing, physiological energy is united with psychological energy and vice-versa. When Pranayama is being done, individual energy is uniting with universal energy (*prana*, energy + *ayama*, expansion).

Cleansing Breath

Ventilates and cleanses the lungs, stimulates the cells and tones respiratory organs. Very refreshing. Sit in meditative posture or stand.
1. Inhale a complete breath.
2. Retain the air for a few seconds.
3. Pucker up the lips as if for a whistle (but do not swell the cheeks), then exhale a little air with vigor. Stop for a moment, retain the air, then exhale a little more air. Repeat until air is completely exhaled. Considerable vigor is to be used in exhaling the air through the opening in the lips.

Deorgha Swasam or Deep Breathing (Complete Breathing)

This complete breathing exercise combines all three portions of the lungs in one continuous full breath. It brings into play the entire respiratory apparatus, every part of the lungs, every part of the air cells, and respiratory muscles.

1. Stand or sit erect. Breathing through the nostrils, inhale steadily, first filling the lower lungs by expanding the stomach (abdominal region), then fill the middle lungs, pushing out the lower ribs, breastbone and chest. In the final movement, the lower part of the abdomen will be slightly drawn in; this movement gives the lungs support and also fills the highest part of the lungs by protruding the upper chest. Practice on one continuous motion.

2. Retain the breath a few seconds.

3. Exhale slowly; first drop the collarbone, then contract the chest and then the stomach in one even motion.

Inhalation begins with the stomach, and exhalation from the top of the lungs. After practice a ratio of 2-4-1 inhalation-holding-exhalation can be used. Two rounds of five each is very beneficial.

Nadi Suddhi or Nerve Purification

Beneficial for shallow breathers, weak hearts; very invigorating. Brings lightness of body, alertness of mind, proper digestion and sound sleep.

Form Vishnu Mudra with the right hand. Close right nostril with thumb, left with ring and little fingers when alternating between nostrils.

1. Inhale through left nostril, right nostril closed with thumb.
2. Close both nostrils (retention of breath).
3. Exhale through right nostril by releasing thumb (left nostril closed).
4. Retain breath (both nostrils closed).
5. Inhale through right nose (left nostril closed).
6. Retain air (both nostrils closed).
7. Exhalation through left nostril (right nostril closed).

This concludes one set. 1 to 2 sets of five is very beneficial.

Kapalabhati or Skull Shining

Expire through both nostrils quickly with an inward abdominal push. Inhale quickly through both nostrils, with relaxation of abdominal wall. Expiration should be continuous and quick. Should start with expiration and end with inspiration. Concentrate. Considered a kriya or cleansing exercise. Cleanses the skull.

Bhastrika or the Bellows Breathing

Do rapid Rechaka and Puraka as in Kapalabhati as many times as is comfortable with slightly extra for Rechaka. When finished, exhale completely and inhale slowly, filling the lungs. Hold the breath, bend the neck, bring chin as close to chest as possible. Retain the breath as long as you can comfortably and then exhale. After exhalation, raise the head up slowly and evenly and exhale through the nose. This is one round of Bhastrika. Do up to your own capacity. Bhastrika brings heat to the body when it is cold. It also helps in curing asthma and consumption, exhilarates the blood and stimulates the entire body.

Sitali or Cooling Breath

Fold the tongue lengthwise like a tube. Project the tip of tongue outside the mouth. Bring in air through the tube with a hissing sound. Fill lungs, bring tongue in, close mouth, and retain air as long as is comfortable. Exhale through the nose. This is one round. Sitali cools the body; it helps to remove heat, hunger and thirst.

It is good to finish Pranayama with a few Complete Breaths. Use your own rhythm, as each person has his or her own rhythm and knows his or her capacity. Pranayama is very good to do just after Asanas and before Dhyana (meditation) as it energizes and brings one to a state of calmness and relaxation.

Sources: Yogi Ramacharaka's Science of Breath; Sri Satchidananda's Integral Yoga Hatha.

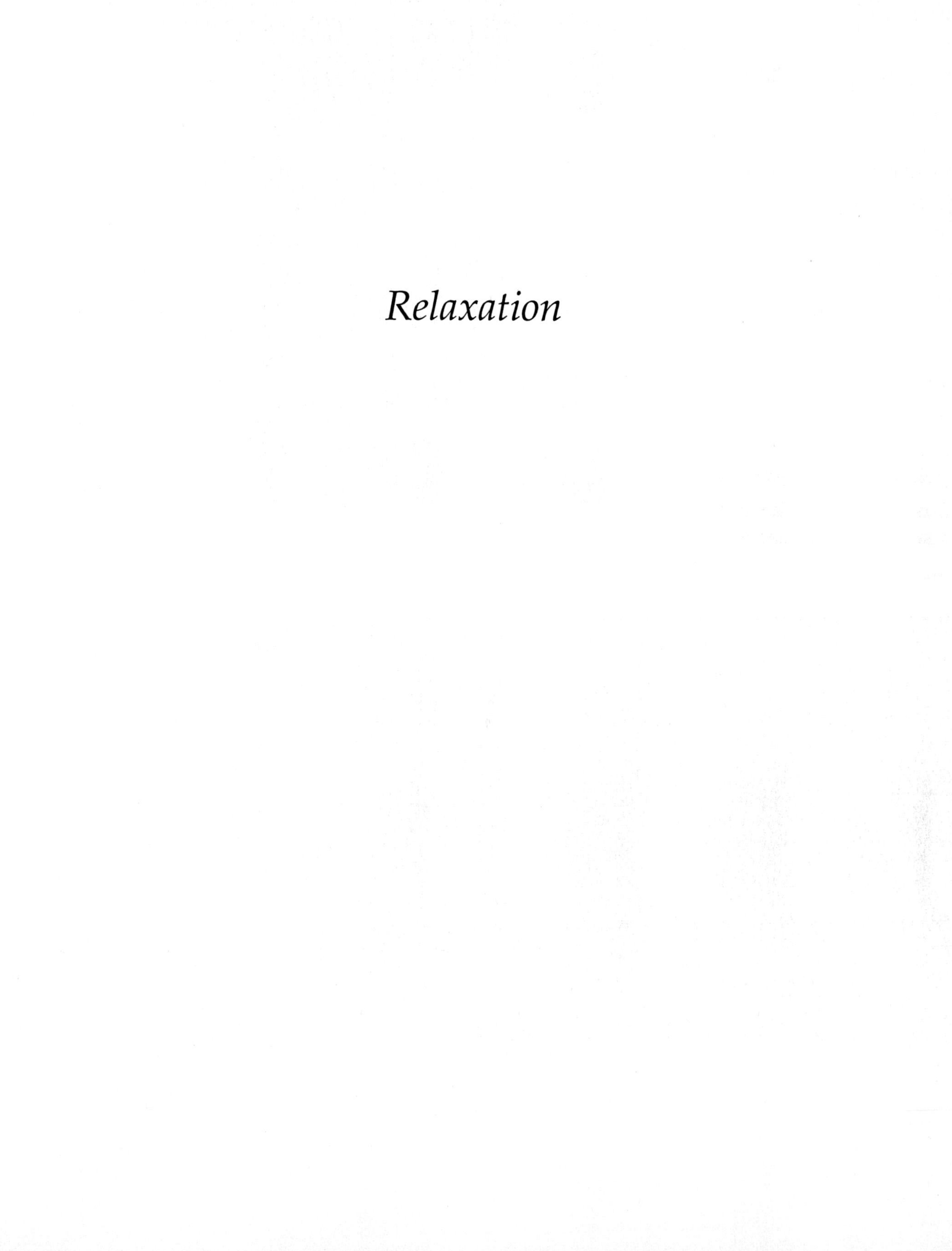

Relaxation

RELAXATION
By Nancy Bessette

Life is constantly changing. With computers and technology, the rate of change has increased dramatically. Stress is constant and cumulative. It is the sum total of the body's breathing patterns. The stress response can be an unconscious habit. It is learned and can be unlearned. We know that over time, our bodies suffer *dis-ease* from holding stress and our spirits lose joyfulness.

Relaxation is a conscious state in which energy is equally dispersed in the body and the mind is at rest. Meditation is when we find the balance of concentrating in a relaxed way and relaxing in a concentrated way. It is not sleep. The idea is to become physically and mentally at peace by not moving and not thinking and then to be there for the experience.

Relaxation and conscious breathing are an integral part of every yoga session. In stillness, we seek out the tension and tightness. Insight is gained as we notice our patterns of holding thoughts and stresses in our bodies. In the postures we stretch and release the tightness from our bodies. Deep breathing techniques direct the mind away from the stress response. One relaxing breath at a time, we build new patterns of being at ease and being in the present moment. One relaxing breath at a time, repeated, builds a foundation for living in a relaxed state. We allow every posture to be a meditation. With each posture, we move toward an inner relaxation with an outer firmness. In slowing down, we respect our body and focus on its wonders. We notice the body's self-healing abilities. The quiet spaces allow us to gain new perceptions that can transform our responses to everyday stresses. The ways we find for mastering a posture apply to mastering situations in life.

Yoga philosophy encourages the student to judge neither himself nor others. In non-doing we can observe, experience, look within and listen. We can sort out what works and what does not work for us. In yoga, we balance doing with non-doing. Daily practice is the key…to persist in practicing daily even when it seems as if it is not working.

WILLIAM'S FLEXION EXERCISES

To be done twice a day, 5 times each as tolerated. Do on firm surface.

1. Pelvic Tilt. Lying on back with knees bent and feet against buttocks, push low back against floor and hold 5 counts & relax.

2. Both Knees to Chest. Roll knees to chest and pull knees to shoulders, lift head and hold 5 counts & relax.

3. Alternate Knee to Chest. Bring R knee to R shoulder, lift head and hold 5 counts (keep L leg straight on floor) & relax. Alternate with L leg.

4. Partial Sit-up. With knees bent, roll pelvis downward as you begin to lift head, stretch hands to knees, hold 5 counts & relax.

THOMPSON'S LOW BACK EXERCISE

Lying on back, draw right ankle to crotch and hold with left hand firmly. Hook right hand around and under right knee, gently rotating right hip outward. Pull down lightly on right knee, towards right elbow. Hold for 60 seconds. Do same to left leg for 60 seconds. Then do right for 30, left for 30 seconds; and then each for 15 seconds. Breathe and be relaxed.

The Asanas

ASANA FUNDAMENTALS

By Nancy Bessette

Yoga means "union" or "joining," the union of the body, mind, and the spirit. Matter, energy, and consciousness are inseparably interrelated. In yoga we take the part of us that thinks, the part of us that wants and feels, and the part of us that acts and attempt to organize and integrate all of these to move in "union" in one direction. The following general principles apply to all of the postures.

IN PREPARATION

- Postures should be done on a fairly firm surface in a well-ventilated room.
- Wear clothing that allows unrestricted movements – comfortably cool or warm.
- Remove most jewelry.
- Use a towel or mat to practice on.
- Refrain from eating heavily at least a couple of hours before you practice.
- Water is essential; drink water when the stomach is empty.
- Avoid caffeine and smoking.

IN PRACTICE

- Yoga is not a competition.... even with yourself .
- Stretching does not equal warm-up...Never bounce or jerk quickly.
- Watch your body temperature...you must be warmed up to stretch.
- Every posture has a "push" and "yield" element. The active force explores the areas of tightness and with the passive force you wait and listen to the body for feedback.
- Put your mind, body, heart, attention, and interest all in one place.
- Observe on the inhale...stretch on the exhale.... pause in stillness in-between.
- Pay attention to the subtle nuances of the process, not just focusing on the end result.
- Begin gradually and progressively ...no matter how fit you are.
- Rest whenever you need to. Resting is an important part of your yoga practice.
- Don't get caught in the trap of thinking you have to be doing all the time...non-doing is also to be practiced.
- When in a posture and at the straining point always back off a little and remain just this side of discomfort...Do not use force...Relax and be gently persistent.
- When doing balancing postures, gaze at a spot somewhere. This will strengthen the eyes as well as still the mind and help the body to balance.
- Practice exact body alignment.
- Keep the breath flowing...Do not hold the breath.
- Always end your practice with the resting pose, becoming silent and relaxed until you are ready to continue your daily activities.
- Mostly remember to be playful and in your attitude!!!

CAUTIONS

Inverted postures should not be practiced by:

- Menstruating women
- Pregnant women
- Persons who are obese or have high risk of heart attack
- Persons with high blood pressure or high cholesterol
- Persons with glaucoma or detached retina
- Persons recovering from eye surgery or under the care of an eye doctor
- Persons with cervical or lumbar injury or malalignment
- Persons who experience pressure in the ears or dizziness

Do not exercise when you are ill, even when you have a "common cold." The body needs rest most of all…not more demands.

Recognize that your limberness and sense of balance will vary from day to day. Your body is affected by how much sleep you are getting, your diet, and how well you cope with stress.

EFFECTS OF POSTURE PRACTICE

STANDING AND BACKBENDING POSTURES - Uplifts the consciousness and builds energy. Gives stability, grounding, and balance. Encourages the active, dynamic life energies or male aspect.

BALANCING POSTURES - Makes the consciousness receptive and sensitive to movement. Centering. Stabilizes the two life energies.

FORWARD BENDING AND INVERTED POSTURES - Calming. Draws you inward. Encourages the passive life energies or female aspects. Reverses the consciousness and circulation. Promotes new and varied perceptions.

TWISTING POSTURES - Stimulates change. Releases tension. Stimulates the spine. Integrates or combines male/female, active/passive, yin/yang energies.

LYING POSTURES - Stills the consciousness. Creates mental relaxation and rest.

Sources for Asana Fundamentals and Postures: Beeken's Yoga of the Heart; Bell's Gentle Yoga; Birch's Power Yoga; Schiffmann's Yoga: Spirit and Practice . . . .

Buddhaprem's Core Postures

BUDDHAPREM'S CORE POSTURES AND PRANAYAMAS

I. **STANDING POSTURES**

A. All Around Stretch
B. Warrior
C. Triangle

II. **BALANCE POSTURES**

A. Stork
B. Tree
C. Eagle

III. **FLOOR POSTURES**

A. Upward / Downward Stretching Dog
B. Knee to Chest
C. Universal Pose

IV. **CLASSIC POSTURES**

A. Forward Bend
B. Spinal Twist
C. Shoulder Stand

V. **PRANAYAMA POSTURES**

A. Complete Breath
B. Fire Breath
C. Alternate Breath

Standing Postures

ALL ROUND STRETCH

- Elongates the body from the inside out
- Develops strength and flexibility to create body balance
- Improves blood circulation and builds heat for other postures
- Stretches spine, shoulders, hips, legs, trunk
- Creates integrated movement by working both sides of body simultaneously with the same depth
- Raises conscious awareness of each body part and of the subtle energies of the body

WARRIOR I & II

- Strengthens legs, hips, ankles
- Stretches waist and rib cage
- Tones all the abdominals
- Creates poise and balance in standing
- Decreases sluggishness and heaviness
- Opens the thymus gland just under the breast bone
- Balances strength, wisdom, love and inner power

REVERSE TRIANGLE

- Relieves back tension
- Tones kidneys
- Works adrenal
- Frees rib cage, chest and heart
- Increases flexibility in the hips, legs, trunk
- Frees energy in the throat center or trust center

Balance Postures

STORK

- Stretches the upper body
- Increases concentration and focus
- Develops balance and body alignment
- Increases strength in the feet, ankles, legs, thighs
- Symbolizes constant flow of energy and matter
- Symbolizes the destruction of the old self in preparation for the creation of the new

TREE

- Loosens hip joints
- Improves posture and balance
- Strengthens legs, ankles, feet
- Increases poise and calmness for all circumstances of life
- Enhances awareness of body-mind interrelatedness

EAGLE

- Creates physical balance
- Strengthens legs, thighs and ankles
- Enhances shoulder flexibility
- Improves awareness of body-mind interrelatedness
- Develops mental concentration and single-mindedness

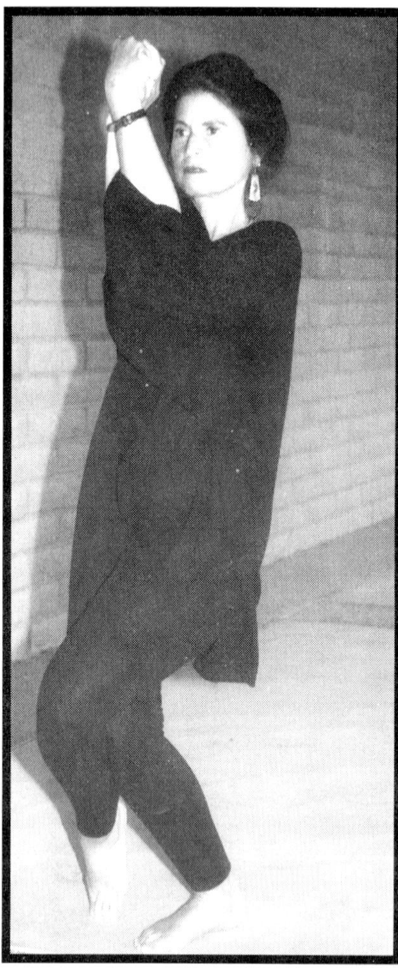

Floor Postures

Up Dog / Down Dog Pose

- Relieves stiff bodies, backaches, tiredness
- Releases spine and hip joints
- Opens shoulders, chest and upper back
- Lengthens the hamstrings
- Strengthens the wrists
- Corrects alignment of major muscles that hold the knees in place
- Strengthens weak or injured knees
- Promotes vitality and aliveness

Knee To Chest

- Rests and eases lower back tension
- Improves circulation in pelvic region
- Opens hips and adductors
- Improves digestion and elimination
- Relieves lower backaches
- Tones abdominal area
- Stretches hamstrings

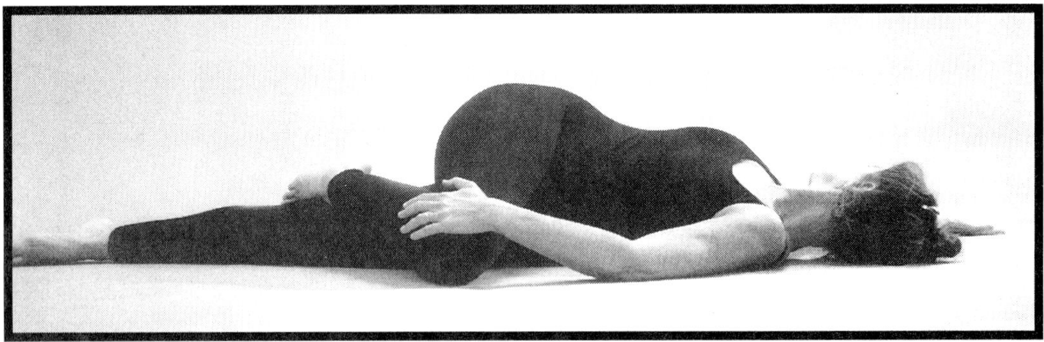

Universal Pose

- Teaches principle of extension during twisting movements
- Eases unevenness in hips, sacrum and lower back
- Corrects spinal alignment
- Slims the waistline
- Releases tension in neck, spine, lower back and hips
- Opens chest and heart

Classic Postures

Forward Bend

- Lengthens and strengthens the spine and hamstrings
- Tones abdominal organs
- Invigorates the nervous system
- Regulates pancreatic function - helpful for those with diabetes or hypoglycemia
- Rests and refreshes the mind and emotions

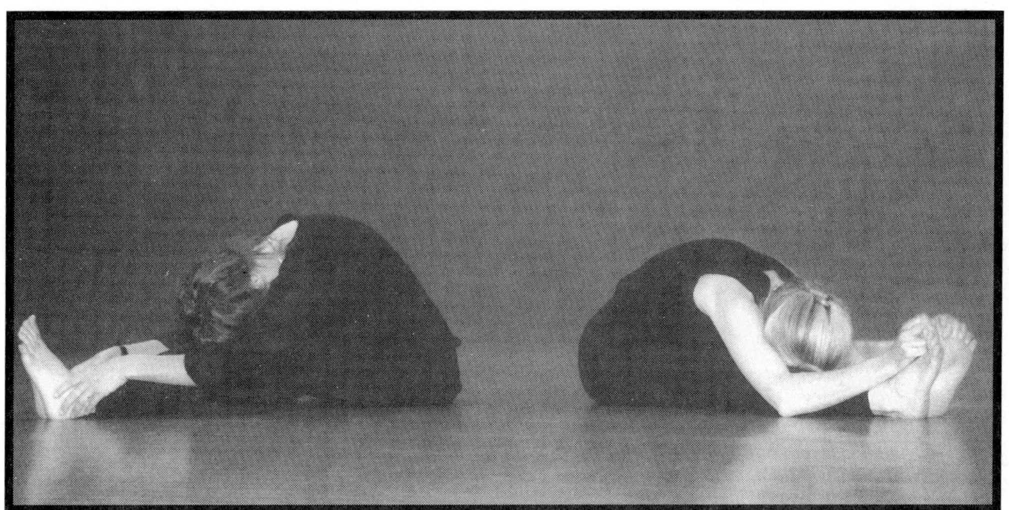

Spinal Twist

- Helps to keep the spine elastic by retaining side to side mobility
- Eases unevenness in the sacrum, hips and lower back
- Helps remove adhesions in the joints caused by rheumatism
- Increases synovial fluid of the joints and makes the joints active
- Releases tension in neck, spine, hips, lower back
- Massages the abdominal muscles relieving digestive problems
- Tones the roots of the spinal nerves and brings blood supply to the area

Shoulder Stand

- Stretches neck, shoulders and upper back
- Relieves fatigue and aids insomnia
- Prevents headaches
- Relieves varicose veins
- Strengthens the legs, buttocks, abdominals
- Helps for insomnia, fatigue, nervous exhaustion
- Increases blood flow to the brain for memory and clearing thoughts
- Gives new perspectives when upside down!

Additional Postures

Expanded Chest/Leg Stretch

- Stretches hamstrings and adductors
- Elongates spin
- Opens chest and heart
- Increases range of motion in shoulders, upper back, neck
- Releases tension in arms,chest, back, shoulders
- Helps prevent rounded shoulders

Standing Forward Bend

- Intensely stretches the backs of legs
- Elongates spine from base to crown
- Increases blood supply to brain
- Tones liver, spleen and kidneys
- Relieves pain during menstruation
- Corrects inequalities in lengths of legs
- Helps the practice of letting go, lengthening and softening

Cat Stretches

- Promotes spinal strength and flexibility
- Teaches how to initiate movements from one's center
- Teaches how to synchronize body movements with the breath
- Improves circulation through the spine
- Stimulates spinal fluid and digestive tract
- Stretches front and back of body
- Releases tension in neck and shoulders

Pigeon Pose

- Opens chest
- Strengthens back
- Relieves sciatica
- Makes lotus easier and safer
- Improves flexibility in legs, hips, thighs

Tip Toe Pose

- This is an advanced balance posture with all of the benefits of Eagle Posture
- Requires increased level of strength, flexi bility, and mental concentration

HEADSTAND

- Increases blood flow to the brain for memory
- Clears thought process
- Rejuvenates all the glands of the endocrine system
- Helps insomnia, fatigue and nervous exhaustion
- Relieves colds, coughs and constipation
- Strengthens arms, shoulders and abdominals
- Gives new perspectives when upside down!

Table

- Improves sluggish digestion
- Breaks up tension
- Strengthens arms, shoulders, buttocks, wrists and legs
- Tones abdomen and spine
- Keeps body alert and mind clear
- Opens heart and chest

WHEEL

- Develops strength and flexibility of spine and whole body
- Massages all the muscles of the back
- Relieves afflictions of the trachea and larynx
- Improves memory and concentration
- Energizing and calming

Seated Angle Pose

- Improves circulation of the pelvic region
- Relaxes spine and hip joints
- Releases the hamstrings and adductors
- Tones liver and kidneys
- Relieves menstrual and menopausal symtoms
- Tones ovaries and prostate
- Aids in digestion

YOGA MUDRA

- Increases circulation in lumbar and abdomen
- Massages the internal organs
- Stretches neck and spine
- Draws attention inward
- Helps in the development of humility

SITTING MEDITATION

Beginning of the Yoga Session

- Increases attention to body alignment and the subtle requests of the body
- Clarifies the purpose and intention of the practice - sets the tone
- Establishes inner attunement to the present moment
- Deepens awareness of the breath

End of the Yoga Session

- Relaxes, refreshes, rejuvenates
- Trains you to be tension-free, undefended, as well as alert
- Gives you time to absorb and integrate the benefits of the other poses
- Improves circulation, regulates blood pressure, reduces fatigue
- Gives experience of calmness and peace

12
1
11
2
10
3
9
4
8
5
7
6
©

SUN SALUTATION

I. Stand erect, palms of hands pressed together against the chest.

II. Inhale, bend back from waist, arms high over head.

III. Exhale, bend forward hands to floor on either side of feet. From this posture try not to move the hands from the floor during the following positions.

IV. Inhale, extend right leg back, keeping left leg in position between hands, stretch head back.

V. Hold breath, extend left leg so body is in a straight line resting on hands and bent toes.

VI. Exhale, lowering the body to rest on eight points, feet, knees, chest, hands & forehead.

VII. Inhale, flatten body to floor and push upper half of body into the Swan position.

VIII. Exhale, lifting hips, legs straight and heels flat on the floor, the body forms a tent.

IX. Inhale, bring right foot forward between hands and stretch back as in Position IV.

X. Exhale, bring left leg next to right and straighten both knees, keeping head down and hands on floor as in Position III.

XI. Inhale, stand up and stretch spine from waist, arms high over head as in Position II.

XII. Exhale, standing erect, palms of hands together as in Position I.

Continue the same routine only extend the left leg back, then left leg forward. When you have done both legs, that constitutes one round.

Basic Program

ELEMENTAL YOGA

By Vincent D. McCullough

Elemental Yoga is an approach to Yoga that allows one to get out of mind and into body. All too often we don't really experience our body. We experience only a thought *about* our body. This "thought kind of " body experience is very thin and sterile, not very juicy and certainly not very satisfying. But if we can re-learn that which we knew as children--to relate to our 'physicalness' directly by relating to the basic core elements of our experience--then we have a chance to feel ourselves at a real concrete level, not diluted and colored by thought.

According to some theories on Tibetan Yoga, we are physically and emotionally comprised of five elements: earth, water, fire, air and space. While practicing Elemental Yoga we can "feel" these different aspects of our nature, allowing us to get in touch with the fundamental physical sensations of our chemical composition. By allowing ourselves to focus and feel these elemental aspects of our nature we can begin to appreciate each individual element. We can feel the active energies of the "fire" in us, we can feel the grounding of "earth," we feel the flow and the cohesion of "water," the expansiveness of "air" and the pervasiveness of "space."

It is through recognizing and nurturing each aspect of our nature that we begin to bring each of these basic elements into the awareness of our being, and it is only through that increased awareness of our being that we can begin to bring all of these elements into balance with each other. Once the elements are in balance they can then begin to vibrate in harmony with each other and ultimately to vibrate in harmony with the universal rhythm of life.

For example, our Earth experience is our experience of gravity. If we don't align successfully with gravity we feel overly contracted, tense, heavy and depressed. But if we learn to make friends with gravity and align successfully, we can then experience our sense of ground that allows us to feel secure, strong and stable.

The next quality of importance is the Water quality of our bodies. If we allow the flow of our bodies to happen and we don't cut it off by undue 'holding', then we can feel that great river of life force smoothly move through our system, connecting each part of us to ourselves. We can then experience the metamorphosis, from feeling frozen to thawing into a stream that widens into a great river and flows into the deep open ocean.

The next quality is Fire. Every cell in our body explodes and releases energy. This explosion and release can be a highly energized process if we allow it. If we learn to breathe correctly and eat correctly, then we can feel the elevation, the warmth, and the light of fire. Correct use of the fire element counteracts the negative aspects of lethargy, heaviness and coldness.

The Air element represents the expansiveness of our nature. Every moment of our life we are experiencing the contraction and expansion of our entire physical system. This is the natural rhythm of life that parallels the great rhythm of the universe. If we get stuck in contraction, with limited possibility for expansion, then we tend to feel pain and physically closed. When we allow ourselves to expand, at least in equal measure, then we tend to feel open, free and expressive.

Then at last we feel Space or Spaciousness. Space is that pervasive quality of just being present or just being here, or put another way, just "being." We feel like an open sky that can never be disturbed, stained or tarnished in any way. We are open, we are everywhere, and we give ourselves room to experience everything completely without negative attachments.

So then, when we feel our physicalness at the elemental level, and when we have rid ourselves of the brain overlay and its busy interpretation of our thoughts and actions (which is often contrived and false); when we feel our body at a real physical level, we are more connected to ourselves as well as to everything else. We then feel good. We even have a chance to feel bliss.

ELEMENTAL YOGA

FIRE

ACTIVE
ENERGETIC
ELEVATION
LIGHT
WARMTH

BREATH:
KAPALABHATI

POSTURES:
STOMACH LIFTS
LEG BENDS
HANDS ON KIDNEYS
RAG DOLL
RUNNING IN PLACE

MUSIC:
TRANSFER STATION BLUES - MICHAEL SHRIEVE
BONES - GABRIELLE ROTH
DEEP BREAKFAST – RAY LYNCH

EARTH

STRENGTH
SOLIDITY
CONTRACTION
GROUND
POWER OF GRAVITY

BREATH:
BHASTRIKA

POSTURES:
TIBETAN RITES OF REJUVENATION:
SPIN CHAKRAS
LEG LIFTS
CAMEL
TABLE
UP DOG/DOWN DOG

MUSIC:
SHAMANIC DREAM - ANUGAMA
MIND DANCE - DANIEL KOBIALKA

ELEMENTAL YOGA

WATER

FLUIDITY
FLOW
COHESION

BREATH:
WATER
BREATHE IN THROUGH NOSE,
OUT THROUGH MOUTH;
HAAA SOUND

POSTURES:
ON FLOOR JOINT WORK:
ANKLE ROLLS
INNER THIGH STRETCH
HIP OPENING
SIMPLE SPINAL TWIST
KNEE TO CHEST
BRIDGE
UNIVERSAL POSE

MUSIC:
MUSICAL MASSAGE (VOL. 2) – RELAXATION COMPANY
SEASHORE INTERLUDES – RISING SUN RECORDS

ELEMENTAL YOGA

AIR

EXPANSION
LIGHT
UPWARD & OUT ENERGY

<u>BREATH:</u>
AIR BREATH
SOFT BREATHING IN & OUT OF MOUTH AT THE SAME TIME

<u>POSTURES:</u>
CLASSIC POSES:
HEAD TO KNEE
ARCHING POSES
COLORA
BOW
LOCUST
YOGA MUDRA
SPINAL TWIST
SHOULDER STAND
FISH

<u>MUSIC:</u>
RAKU - P.C. DAVIDOFF & FRIENDS
MUSIC TO DISAPPEAR IN - RAPHAEL

ELEMENTAL YOGA

SPACE

PERVASIVENESS
EVERYWHERENESS

BREATH:
AIR BREATH
VERY SHALLOW,
ALMOST A SUSPENSION OF BREATH

POSTURES:
RESTING POSE

MUSIC:
RAKU - P.C. DAVIDOFF & FRIENDS
MUSIC TO DISAPPEAR IN - RAPHAEL

1. Larynx
2. Thyroid
3. Esophagus
4. Lungs
5. Heart
6. Liver
7. Stomach
8. Spleen
9. Pancreas
10. Kidneys
11. Transverse colon
12. Ascending colon
13. Descending colon
14. Small intestine
15. Uterus
16. Ovary
17. Bladder
18. Testicles
19. Prostate glands
20. Diaphragm

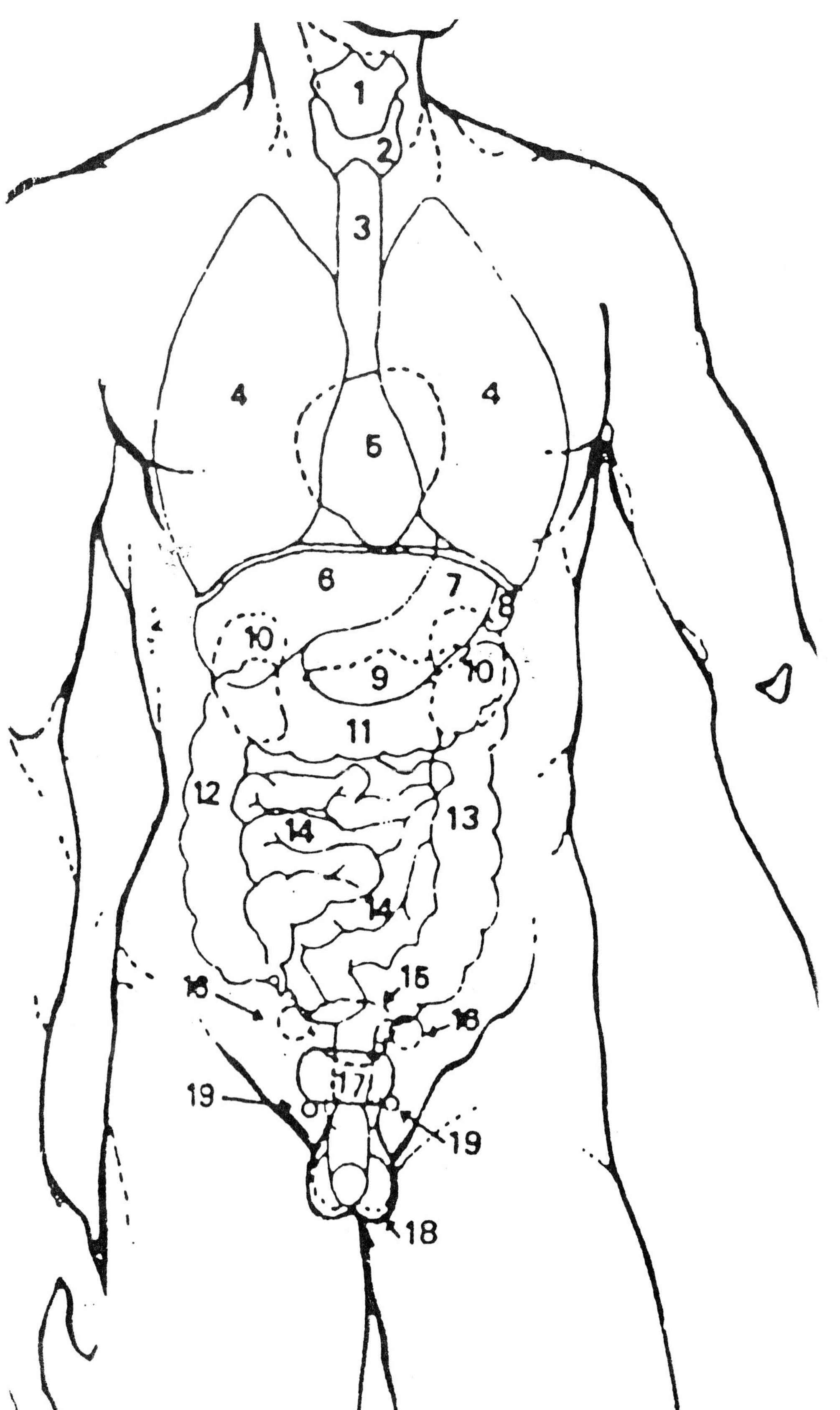

PHYSICAL LIFE CENTERS

As we have learned, the classic postures of yoga along with appropriate visualizations and pranayamas deeply affect the life centers of the body; these correspond to the regions controlled by the endocrine glands. (See chart p. 131.) The intent of yoga is to balance the glandular system, align the spine, activate the plexus, and exercise the organs. (See chart p. 202.) This emphasizes the physical work of yoga.

1. *Mobility.* An irritability and conductivity which encourages a contact with the environment to take place, and the elimination of unwanted energy.

2. *A reproductive system that furthers life* and establishes contact on the physical plane.

3. *A digestive system* that takes in food energy, and redistributes from it what is necessary for the growth of the organism.

4. *A vitalizing (circulatory) process.* This is the heart of the organism that gives the will to live by virtue of its magnetizing or attracting force.

5. *A metabolic (respiratory) controlling mechanism* that keeps a balance of the above four functions.

6. *Contractability.* A nervous system gives the cell the ability to go within itself. A sort of instinctive or intuitive knowing element feeds information to all parts of the cell and controls its automatic responses.

7. *Adaptability.* A nervous system which enables the cell to survive in changing environmental conditions. This is like a creative image-making faculty that forms new patterns for future cells.

Source: Malcolm Strutt's Wholistic Health and Living Yoga.

Meditation

DHARANA (ONE-POINTEDNESS): Or, The Key To Doing Yoga Well

By Vincent D. McCullough

Doing well in yoga does not mean standing on your head, sitting in the Lotus position or putting your chin beyond your knees in forward stretching pose. Rather, doing well in yoga is practicing and achieving some mastery of the Dharana principle.

DHARANA – (DESA-BANDHAS-CITTASYA-DHARANA)
Concentration is the focusing and binding of consciousness to a single point. This focus on a single object is a nonthinking one-pointedness of the mind. Long ago Swami Vivekananda noted: "Take up one idea. Make that one idea your life—think of it, dream of it, live on that one idea. Let the brain, muscles, nerves, every part of your body be full of that idea, and just leave every other idea alone."

In plainer terms, when you practice yoga let your mind focus on one point. The point might be your posture; it might be your breath, it might be a body sensation or it might be wherever your awareness is at that moment. But whatever your point of awareness is, focus on it and bind to it.

The power then inherent in this act of awareness is the power to take you more deeply into form, in an attempt to arrive at that which lies behind the form or to reach the idea which is responsible for the form.

In other words, this act of one-pointed concentration can let you discover the deeper less surface or obvious principles of yoga. While Asana and Pranayama mastery without Dharana is adequate and perhaps in some physical aspect fine, it will still lack true revelation and understanding.

When Dharana is sustained, it becomes Dhyana (Meditation), and that is the ultimate key to 'self perfection'. Meditation is best summed up by Christmas Humphreys:

> The main purpose of Meditation is contained in the word alignment, a deliberate opening of the higher faculties in order that each aspect of our complex being may become enlightened. A lesser, but equally essential service rendered by this practice may be described as spiritual digestion, a distillation of wisdom from the fruits of experience. This involves a periodic withdrawal from the outer into the inner world for silent communion with the highest one, for here alone values may be understood. Here is the navigator's chart of yet untravelled seas, the plans of the architect whose actual building has scarce left the cradle of his dreams, the searchlight of a faculty whose light alone will pierce the darkness of the path ahead. Truly he travels blind who does not meditate!

Sources: Bailey's The Light of the Soul; Humphrey's Concentration and Meditation; Swami Vivekananda's Raja-Yoga.

KEEPING STILL

Keeping still. Keeping his back still
So that he no longer feels his body.
He goes into his courtyard
And does not see his people.
No blame.

[The commentary reads:] True quiet means keeping still when it is time to keep still, and going forward when the time has come to go forward. In this way movement and rest are in agreement with the demands of the time, and thus there is light in life.

The hexagram signifies the end and beginning of all movement. The back is named because in the back are located all the nerve fibers that mediate movement. If the movement of these spinal nerves is brought to a standstill, the ego, with its restlessness, disappears as it were. When a man has thus become calm, he may turn to the outside world. He no longer sees in it the struggle and tumult of individual beings, and therefore he has that true peace of mind which is needed for understanding the great laws of the universe and for acting in harmony with them. Whoever acts from these deep levels makes no mistakes.

The I Ching, or Book of Changes, ed. Richard Wilhelm

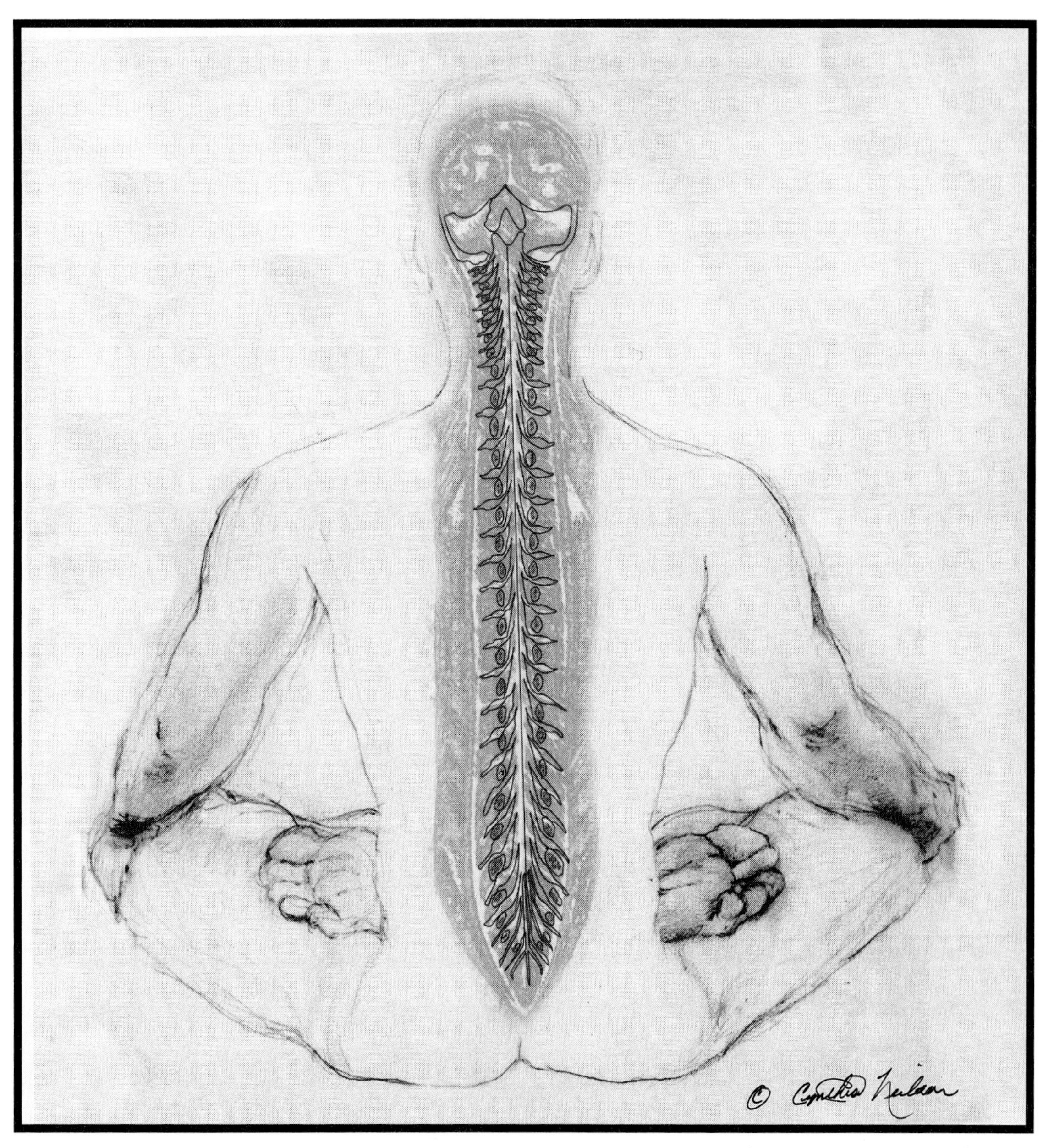

Epilogue: The Ten Bulls

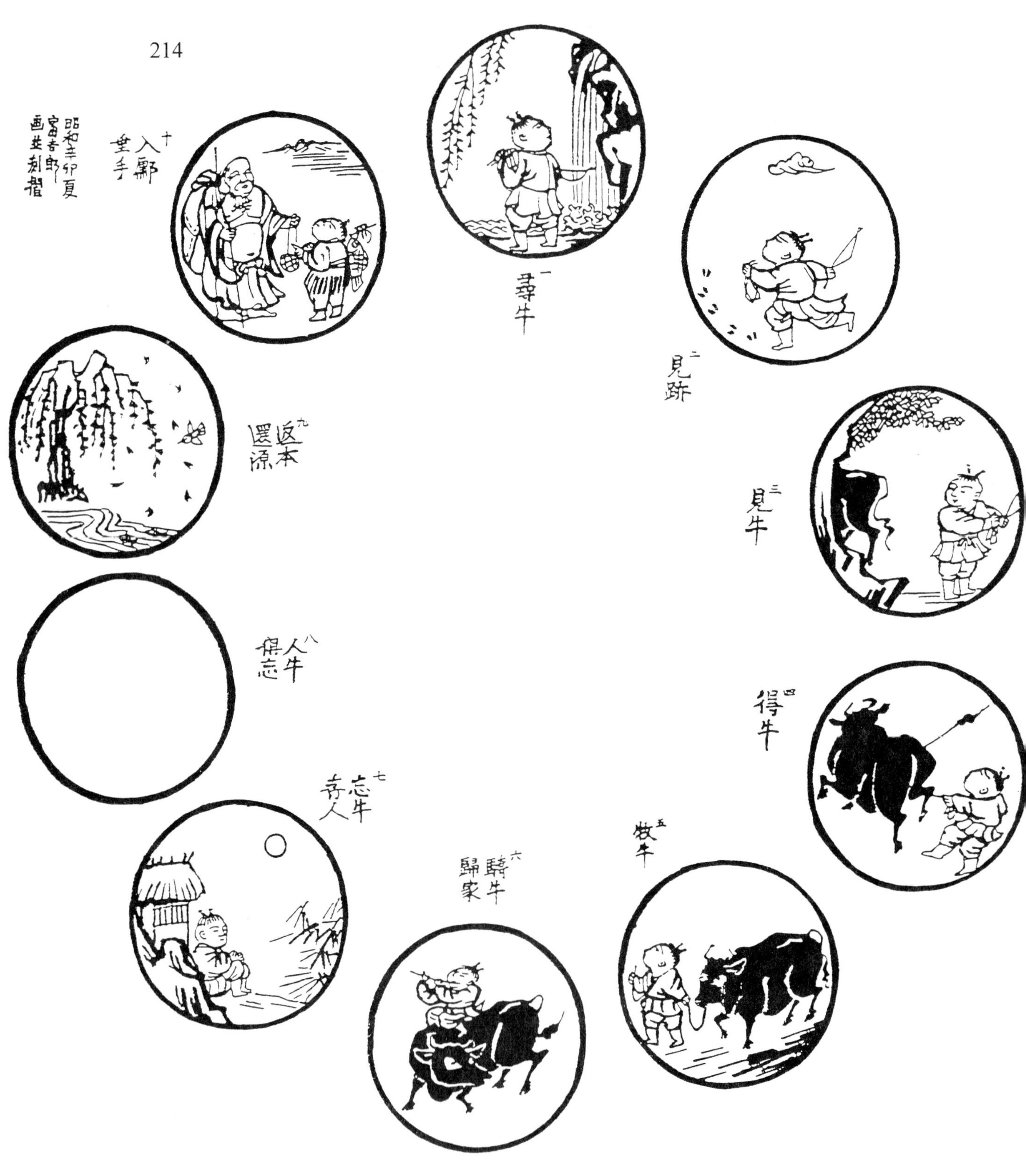

The Ten Bulls

EPILOGUE: THE TEN BULLS

The most profound yet simplest link between Yoga and Aikido (Zen) lies at the heart of the ten oxherding pictures. These timeless paintings originated with the 12th century Chinese master Kakuan, who based them on earlier Taoist bulls. He accompanied them with comments in poetry and prose, translated by Paul Reps and Nyogen Senzaki. Noted Kyoto woodblock artist Tomikichiro Tokuriki has reproduced the pictures we have today.

We have both been long familiar with the pictures. So it was no great surprise to find them in each other's syllabus, serving as a microcosm for our purpose as teachers and travelers along life's path. We would like for them to make the final comment to our text, prefaced by the words of Reps and Senzaki in Zen Flesh, Zen Bones:

> The bull is the eternal principle of life, truth in action. The ten bulls represent sequent steps in the realization of one's true nature.
>
> This sequence is as potent today as it was when Kakuan (1100-1200) developed it from earlier works and made his paintings of the bull. Here in America we perform a similar work eight centuries later to keep the bull invigorated. . . .
>
> An understanding of the creative principle transcends any time or place. The Ten Bulls is more than poetry, more than pictures. It is a revelation of spiritual unfoldment paralleled in every bible of human experience. May the reader, like the Chinese patriarch, discover the footprints of his potential self and, carrying the staff of his purpose and the wine jug of his true desire, frequent the market place and there enlighten others.

1. The Search for the Bull

In the pasture of this world, I endlessly push aside the tall grasses in search of the bull.
Following unnamed rivers, lost upon the interpenetrating paths of distant mountains,
My strength failing and my vitality exhausted, I can not find the bull.

2. Discovering the Footprints

Along the riverbank under the trees, I discover footprints!
Even under the fragrant grass I see his prints.
Deep in the remote mountains they are found.
These traces no more can be hidden than one's nose, looking heavenward.

3. Perceiving the Bull

I hear the song of the nightingale.
The sun is warm, the wind is mild, willows are green along thc shore.
Here the Bull can hide!
What artist can draw that massive head, those majestic horns?

4. Catching the Bull

I seize him with a terrific struggle.
His great will and power are inexhaustible.
He charges to the high plateau far above the cloud-mists,
Or in an impenetrable ravine he stands.

5. Taming the Bull

The whip and rope are necessary,
Else he might stray off down some dusty road.
Being well trained, he becomes naturally gentle.
Then, unfettered, he obeys his master

6. Riding the Bull Home

Mounting the bull, slowly I return homeward.
The voice of my flute intones through the evening.
Measuring with hand-beats the pulsating harmony, I direct the endless rhythm.
Whoever hears this melody will join me.

7. The Bull Transcended

Astride the bull, I reach home.
I am serene. The bull too can rest.
The dawn has come. In blissful repose,
Within my thatched dwelling I have abandon the whip and rope.

8. Both Bull and Self Transcended

Whip, rope, person, and bull - all merge in No-Thing.
This heaven is so vast no message can stain it.
How may a snowflake exist in a raging fire?
Here are the footprints of the patriarchs.

9. Reaching the Source

Too Many steps have been taken returning to the root and the source.
Better to have been blind and deaf from the beginning!
Dwelling in one's true abode, unconcerned with that without -
The river flows tranquilly on and the flowers are red.

10. In the World

Bare footed and naked of breast, I mingle with the people of the world.
My clothes are ragged and dust-laden, and I am ever blissful.
I use no magic to extend my life;
Now, before me, the dead trees become alive.

1. The Search for the Bull
Comment: The bull never has been lost. What need is there to search? Only because of separation from my true nature, I fail to find him. In the confusion of the senses I lose even his tracks. Far from home, I see many crossroads, but which way is the right one I know not. Greed and fear, good and bad, entangle me.

2. Discovering the Footprints
Comment: Understanding the teaching, I see the footprints of the bull. Then I learn that, just as many utensils are made from one metal, so too are myriad entities made of the fabric of self. Unless I discriminate, how will I perceive the true from the untrue? Not yet having entered the gate, nevertheless I have discerned the path.

3. Perceiving the Bull
Comment: When one hears the voice, one can sense its source. As soon as the six senses merge, the gate is entered. Wherever one enters one sees the head of the bull! This unity is like salt in water, like color in dyestuff. The slightest thing is not apart from self.

4. Catching the Bull
Comment: He dwelt in the forest a long time, but I caught him today! Infatuation for scenery interferes with his direction. Longing for sweeter grass, he wanders away. His mind still is stubborn and unbridled. If I wish him to submit, I must raise my whip.

5. Taming the Bull
Comment: When one thought arises, another thought follows. When the first thought springs from enlightenment, all subsequent thoughts are true. Through delusion, one makes everything untrue. Delusion is not caused by objectivity; it is the result of subjectivity. Hold the nose-ring tight and do not allow even a doubt.

6. Riding the Bull Home
Comment: This struggle is over; gain and loss are assimilated. I sing the song of the village woodsman, and play the tunes of the children. Astride the bull, I observe the clouds above. Onward I go, no matter who may wish to call me back.

7. The Bull Transcended
Comment: All is one law, not two. We only make the bull a temporary subject. It is as the relation of rabbit and trap, of fish and net. It is as gold and dross, or the moon emerging from a cloud. One path of clear light travels on throughout endless time.

8. Both Bull and Self Transcended
Comment: Mediocrity is gone. Mind is clear of limitation. I seek no state of enlightenment. Neither do I remain where no enlightenment exists. Since I linger in neither condition, eyes cannot see me. If hundreds of birds strew my path with flowers, such praise would be meaningless.

9. Reaching the Source
Comment: From the beginning, truth is clear. Poised in silence, I observe the forms of integration and disintegration. One who is not attached to "form" need not be "reformed." The water *is* emerald, the mountain *is* indigo, and I see that which *is* creating and that which *is* destroying.

10. In the World
Comment: Inside my gate, a thousand sages do not know me. The beauty of my garden is invisible. Why should one search for the footprints of the patriarchs? I go to the market place with my wine bottle and return home with my staff. I visit the wineshop and the market, and everyone I look upon becomes enlightened.

Bibliography

WORLD WIDE WEB RESOURCES

Aikido/Aikibujutsu Page
http://www.shinkendo.com/aikido.html

Aikido Federation (PAF-Pacific Aikido Federation)
http://www.schillace.com/aikido/paf.htm

Aikido Philosophy
http://ee.ogi.edu/omlc/aikido/talk/

AikiWeb
http://www.aikiweb.com/

Body Mind & Modem
http://www.bodymindandmodem.com/

Oregon Graduate Institute Aikido
http://ee.ogi.edu/omlc/aikido/index.html

PUBLICATIONS

Aikido Journal Online
http://www-cse.ucsd.edu/users/paloma/Aikido/AJ/atm/

Aikido Today Magazine
http://www.cyberg8t.com/

Furyu Online - Budo Journal of Classical Japanese Martial Arts
http://www.furyu.com/

ZEN

Abe, Maseo. Zen and Western Thought. Honolulu, HI: University of Hawaii Press, 1985.

Aitken, Robert. A Zen Wave: Basho's Haiku & Zen. New York: Weatherhill, 1979.

Aitken, Robert. Encouraging Words: Zen Buddhist Teachings for Western Students. New York: Pantheon Books, 1994.

Aitken, Robert. The Gateless Barrier : The Wu-Men Kuan. San Francisco: North Point Press, 1991.

Aitken, Robert. The Practice of Perfection: The Paramitas from a Zen Buddhist Perspective. Washington, DC: Counterpoint, 1997.

Aoyama, Shundo. Zen Seeds: Reflections of a Female Priest, trans. Patricia Daien Bennage. Boston: Charles E. Tuttle, 1990

Austin, James H. Zen and the Brain: Toward an Understanding of Meditation and Consciousness. Cambridge, MA: MIT Press, 1998.

Baldock, John. The Little Book Of Zen Wisdom. Shaftesbury, Dorset; Rockport, MA: Element, 1994.

Barret, William. Zen Buddhism: Selected Writings of D.T. Suzuki. New York: Doubleday, 1996.

Baxter, Joan. Sword of No Blade. York Beach, ME: Samuel Weiser, 1992.

Beck, Charlotte Joko. Nothing Special: Living Zen. Ed. Steve Smith. New York: Harper, 1994.

Blackman, Sushila. ed. Graceful Exits: How Great Beings Die: Death Stories of Tibetan, Hindu & Zen Masters. New York: Weatherhill, 1997.

Bodri, William, and Lee Shu-Mei. Twenty-Five Doors To Meditation: A Handbook For Entering Samadhi. York Beach, ME: Samuel Weiser, 1998.

Chang, Chen-Chi. Practice of Zen. New York: Harper, 1959.

Chen, Kaiguo, and Zheng Shunchao. Opening the Dragon Gate: The Making of a Taoist Wizard, trans. Thomas Cleary. Boston: Charles E. Tuttle, 1996.

Ch'ing-yuan. Instant Zen: Waking up in the Present. Trans. Thomas Cleary. Berkeley, CA: North Atlantic Books, 1994.

Chu-ko, Liang, and Chi Liu. Mastering The Art Of War, trans. and Ed. Thomas Cleary. Boston: Shambhala, 1995.

Chung, Tsai Chih. Zen Speaks: Shouts of Nothingness, trans. Brian Bruya. New York: Anchor, 1994.

Cleary, Thomas. ed. Kensho: The Heart of Zen. Trans. Thomas Cleary. Boston: Shambhala; New York: Dist. in U.S. by Random House, 1997.

Cleary, Thomas. ed. Teachings of Zen, trans. Thomas Cleary. Boston: Shambhala; New York: Dist. in the U.S. by Random House, 1998.

Deshimaru, Taisen. Questions to a Zen Master, trans. Nancy Amphourx. New York: Penguin Books, 1991.

Deshimaru, Taisen. Sit: Zen Teachings of Master Taisen Deshimaru. Ed. Phillippe Coupey. Prescott, AZ: Hohm Press, 1996.

Dogen, Eihei and Kazuaki Tanahashi, ed. Moon in a Dewdrop: Writings of Zen Master Dogen. San Francisco: North Point Press, 1995.

Fisher-Schreiber, Ingrid et al. eds. The Encyclopedia of Eastern Philosophy and Religion: Buddhism, Hinduism, Taoism, Zen. Boston: Shambhala, 1994.

Furuya, Kensho. Kodo Ancient Ways: Lessons in the Spiritual Life of the Warrior/Martial Artist. Santa Clarita, CA: Ohara Publications, 1996.

Gak, Dae. Going Beyond Buddha: The Awakening Practice of Listening. Boston: Charles E. Tuttle, 1997.

Grigg, Ray. The Tao of Zen. Boston: Charles E. Tuttle, 1994.

Hakuin. Zen Words for the Heart: Hakuin's Commentary on the Heart Sutra. Trans. Norman Waddell. Boston: Shambhala, 1996.

Herrigel, Eugene. Zen in the Art of Archery. New York: Vintage Books, 1989.

Huai-Chin, Nan. Basic Buddhism: Exploring Buddhism And Zen. York Beach, Me: Samuel Weiser, 1997.

Hui-k'ai. Unlocking The Zen Koan : A New Translation Of The Zen Classic Wumenguan, trans. Thomas Cleary. Berkeley, CA: North Atlantic Books, 1997.

Hui-neng. The Sutra of Hui-neng, Grand Master of Zen, trans. Thomas Cleary. Boston: Shambhala, 1998.

Kapleau, Philip, ed. The Three Pillars of Zen: Teaching, Practice, and Enlightenment. New York: Anchor Books, 1989.

Leggett, Trevor. Three Ages of Zen: Samurai, Feudal, and Modern. Boston: Charles E. Tuttle, 1993.

Leggett, Trevor. ed. The Tiger's Cave and Translations of Other Zen Writings. Boston, Charles E. Tuttle, 1995.

Myokyo-ni. The Zen Way. Boston: Charles E. Tuttle, 1995.

Nhat Hanh, Thich. The Miracle of Mindfulness : A Manual on Meditation. Boston: Beacon Press, 1992.

Reps, Paul. Zen Flesh, Zen Bones. New York: Doubleday, 1957.

Sekida, Katsuki. Two Zen Classics: Mumonkan and Hekiganroku. Ed. A.V. Grimstone. New York: Weatherhill, 1995.

Sidor, Ellen. ed. A Gathering of Spirit: Women Teaching in American Buddhism. Cumberland, RI: Primary Point Press, 1992.

Suzuki , Daisetz Teitaro. Buddha of Infinite Light. Boston: Shambhala, 1998.

Suzuki, D.T. The Zen Doctrine Of No-Mind. York Beach, ME: Samuel Weiser, 1993.

Suzuki, D.T. The Zen Koan As a Means of Attaining Enlightenment. Boston: Charles E. Tuttle, 1994.

Tanahashi, Kazuaki, and David Schneider. eds. Essential Zen. San Francisco: HarperCollins, 1995.

Tao-yuan, Shih. The Transmission of The Lamp: Early Masters. Trans. Sohaku Ogata. Wolfeboro, NH: Longwood Academic, 1989.

Tohei, Koichi. Aikido in Daily Life. Trans. Richard L. Gage. Tokyo: Rikuge Publishing House, 1966.

Waddell, Norman. The Essential Teachings of Zen Master Hakuin; A Translation of the Sikko-Roku Kaien-Fusetsu. Boston: Shambhala, 1994.

Watts, Alan. The Way of Zen. New York: Pantheon, 1957.

WORLD WIDE WEB RESOURCES

Alan Watts Electronic University
http://www.alanwatts.com/

American Zen Association
http://www.gnofn.org/~aza/

AZI: International Zen Association
http://www.zen-azi.org/

WWW Virtual Library - Zen Buddhism
http://www.ciolek.com/WWWVL-Zen.html

The Zen Studies Society
http://www.zenstudies.org/

Zen Center of Los Angeles
http://www.zencenter.com/

Reps, Paul. Zen Flesh, Zen Bones. New York: Doubleday, 1957.

Russell, Edward W. Design for Destiny. New York: Ballantine Books, 1971.

Satchidananda, Sri S. Integral Yoga Hatha. Henry Holt & Co., 1970.

Schiffmann, Erich, Yoga: The Spirit and Practice Of Moving Into Stillness. New York: Pocket Books, New York, 1996.

Strutt, Malcolm. Wholistic Health and Living Yoga. Boulder Creek, CA: University of Trees Press, 1977.

Van Lysebeth, Andre. Pranayama: The Yoga of Breathing. London: Mandala Books; Unwin Paperbacks, 1979.

Vishnudevananda, Swami. The Complete Illustrated Book of Yoga. New York: Julian Press, 1960.

Vivekananda, Swami. Raja Yoga, Calcutta, India: 18th printing: Advaita Ashrama, 1982.

White, Ganga. "The Four Yogas." Santa Barbara, CA: White Lotus Foundation, 1990.

Wilhelm, R., ed. The I Ching or Book of Changes, trans. by C.F. Baynes. Princeton University Press, 1967.

Worthington, Vivian. A History of Yoga. London, Boston, Melbourne, Oxon: Routledge & Kegan Paul Ltd., 1982.

FURTHER READINGS

YOGA

Aurobindo, Sri Ghose. Bases Of Yoga. Twin Lakes, WI: Lotus Light, 1993.

Beeken, Jenny. Yoga of the Heart. White Eagle Publishing Trust, 1990.

Birch, Beryl Bender. Power Yoga: The Total Strength and Flexibility Workout. New York: Simon and Schuster, 1995.

Capra, Fritjof. The Tao of Physics. New York: Bantam Books, 1975.

Christensen, Alice. The American Yoga Association's New Yoga Challenge: Powerful Workouts For Flexibility, Strength, Energy, and Inner Discovery. Lincolnwood, IL: Contemporary Books, 1997.

Dworkis, Sam. Recovery Yoga: A Practical Guide for Chronically Ill, Injured, and Post-Operative People. New York: Three Rivers Press, 1997.

Eliade, Mircia. Yoga, Immortality and Freedom. Princeton, NJ: Princeton University Press, 1970.

Ellis, George, and Gina R. Gross. The Breath Of Life: Mastering The Breathing Techniques Of Pranayama And Qigong. New York: Newcastle, 1993.

Feuerstein, Georg. Teachings of Yoga. Boston: Shambhala, 1997.

Feuerstein, Georg. The Yoga-Sutras of Patanjali. Rochester, Vermont: Inner Traditions International, 1979.

Feuerstein, Georg. The Yoga Tradition. Prescott, AZ: Hohm Press, 1998.

Francina, Suza. The New Yoga for People Over 50: A Comprehensive Guide for Midlife and Older Beginners. Deerfield Beach, FL: Health Communications, Inc., 1997.

Ghosh, Shyam. The Original Yoga. New Delhi: Munishiram

Hewitt, James. The Complete Yoga Book: Yoga of Breathing, Yoga of Posture, and Yoga of Meditation/Three Volumes in One. New York: Schocken Book, 1990.

Hirschi, Gertrud. Basic Yoga For Everyone. York Beach, ME: Samuel Weiser, 1998.

Hittleman, Richard. Introduction to Yoga. New York and Toronto: Bantam Books, 1969.

Iyengar, B. K. S., and Yhudi Menuhin. Light on Yoga: Yoga Dipika. New York: Schocken Books, 1995.

Janakananda Saraswati, Swami. Yoga, Tantra and Meditation. York Beach, ME: Samuel Weiser, 1975.

Jones, Annie. Yoga: A Step-By-Step Guide. Shaftesbury, Dorset; Rockport, MA: Element Books, 1998.

Kuvalayananda, Swami. Pranayama. Lonvala, India: Yogi Mimansa Publications, 1965.

Mehta, Mira. How to Use Yoga: A Step-By-Step Guide to the Iyengar Method of Yoga, For Relaxation, Health and Well-Being. Ed. Elaine Collins. New York: Rodnell Press, 1998.

Mishra, Rammurti S., M.D. Fundamentals of Yoga. Garden City, NY: Anchor Press/Doubleday, 1974.

Mohan, A.G. Yoga for Body, Breath and Mind. Cambridge, Mass.: Rudra Press, 1993.

Mumford, Jonn. A Chakra & Kundalini Workbook: Psycho-Spiritual Techniques for Health, Rejuvenation, Psychic Powers And Spiritual Realization. St. Paul, MN: Llewellyn, 1995.

Pandit, M. P. Kundalini Yoga. Twin Lakes, WI: Lotus Light, 1997.

Pratap, Vijayendra. Beginning Yoga. Boston: Charles E. Tuttle, 1997.

Ramacharaka, Yogi. Hatha Yoga. Chicago: Yogi Publications, 1930.

Rush, Anne Kent. The Modern Book of Stretching: Strength and Flexibility at Any Age. New York: Dell, 1997.

Sinh, Pancham. The Hatha Yoga Pradipika. New Delhi: Munishiram Publishers Ltd. 3rd ed., 1980.

Singh, Jaideva. Vijnanabhairava. New Delhi: Motilal Banareidass Publishers Ltd., 1979.

Sivananda Radha, Swami. Kundalini Yoga for the West. Boulder, CO: Shamballa, 1978.

Sivananda Yoga Vedanta Center. The Sivananda Companion to Yoga. New York: Fireside Books, Simon and Schuster, 1983.

Sivananda Yoga Vedanta Center. Yoga: Mind & Body. New York: DK Publishing, Inc., 1996.

Smith, Bob and Linda Boudreau. Yoga for a New Age. Seattle, WA: Smith Productions, 1986.

Strutt, Malcolm. Wholistic Health and Living Yoga. Boulder Creek, CO: University of the Trees Press, 1976.

Taimni, J.K. The Science of Yoga. Wheaton, IL: A Quest Book, The Theosophical Publishing House, 1967.

Vishnudevananda, Swami. The Complete Illustrated Book of Yoga. Julian Press, NY, 1960.

White, John. Kundalini, Evolution and Enlightenment. Paragon House, NY, 1990.

Wilhelm, R., ed. The I Ching or Book of Changes, trans. by C.F. Baynes. Princeton University Press, 1967.

PHILOSOPHY, PSYCHOLOGY, MOTIVATIONAL

Anodea, Judith. Eastern Body, Western Mind: Psychology and the Chakra System. Berkeley, CA: Celestial Arts, 1996.

Anodea, Judith. Wheels of Life. St. Paul, MN: Lluwellyn Press, 1988.

Aurobindo, Sri Ghose. The Upanishads. Twin Lakes, WI: Lotus Light, 1996.

Blum, Ralph H. The Book of Runes. New York: St. Martin's Press, 1993.

Bohm, Werner. Chakras, Yoga and Consciousness: Balancing Your Life. York Beach, ME: Samuel Weiser, 1998.

Borysenko, Joan. Minding the Body, Mending the Soul. New York: Bantam Books, 1987.

Bouanchaud, Bernard. The Essence of Yoga: Reflections on the Yoga Sutras of Patanjali. Trans. Rosemary Desneux. Portland, OR: Rudra International, 1997.

Brennan, Barbara Ann. Light Emerging. New York: Bantam Books, 1993.

Caddy, Eileen. Footprints on the Path. Moray, Scotland: Findhorn Press, 1991.

Feuerstein, Georg. The Essence Of Yoga: Essays On The Development Of Yogic Philosophy From The Vedas To Modern Times. Rochester, VT: Inner Traditions, 1998.

Fisher, Robert. "The Knight in Rusty Armor." 12015 Sherman Rd., Hollywood, CA 1(818)765-8575.

Hayward, Susan. Begin it Now: A Guide for the Advanced Soul. Australia: In Tune Books, 1988.

Huber, Cheri. The Key: And the Name of the Key is Willingness. Center for Zen Meditation, 1990.

Jeffers, Susan. Thoughts of Power and Love. CA: Hayhouse, 1995.

Kabat-Zinn, Jon. Wherever You Go, There You Are. New York: Hyperion, 1994.

Kriyananda, Goswami. Intermediate Guide to Meditation. Chicago: Temple of Kriya Yoga, 1995.

MacIvor, Virginia and Sandra LaForest. Vibrations: Healing through Color, Homeopathy and Radionics. York Beach, ME: Samuel Weiser, Inc., 1979.

Millman, Dan. The Laws Of Spirit: Simple, Powerful Truths for Making Life Work. Tiburon, CA: H.J. Kramer, 1995.

Motoyama, Hiroshi. Theories of the Chakras. Wheaton, IL: A Quest Book, 1981.

Myss, Caroline. Anatomy of the Spirit. New York: Harmony Books, 1996.

Myss, Caroline. Why People Don't Heal and How They Can. New York: Harmony Books, 1997.

Peck, M. Scott. The Road Less Traveled. New York: Simon & Schuster, 1978.

Russell, Edward W. Design for Destiny. New York: Ballantine Books, 1971.

Tobin, Bob, ed. Space – Time and Beyond. New York: Dutton and Co., 1975.

Wing, R.L. The I Ching Workbook. New York: Doubleday, 1979.

Wolf, Fred Allan. Taking the Quantum Leap. New York: Harper and Row, 1986.

Yogananda, Paramahansa. Metaphysical Meditations. Los Angeles: Self-Realization Fellowship, 1997.

Zukav, Gary. The Dancing Wu Li Masters. New York: Bantam Books, 1983.

Zukav, Gary. The Seat of the Soul. New York: Simon & Schuster, 1990.

NUTRITION

Gershoff, Stanley, Ph.D. The Tufts University Guide to Total Nutrition. Harper Perennial, 1996.

Rector-Page, Linda, N.D., Ph. D. Healthy Healing: An Alternative Healing Reference. Healthy Healing Publications, 1998.

WORLD WIDE WEB RESOURCES

American Yoga
http://www.mantra.com.ar/Ingles/americanyoga.html

Self-Realization Fellowship: International Headquarters
http://www.yogananda-srf.org/

The Yoga Center of California
http://www.yogacenter.org/

The Yoga Solution
http://www.yogasolution.com/menu.html

The Yoga Tree of Seattle
http://www.yogatree.com/

Yoga Internet Resources
http://www.holisticmed.com/www/yoga.html

Yoga Research Foundation
http://www.yrf.org/

Yoga Site
http://www.yogasite.com/

PUBLICATIONS

Yoga Journal's YogaNet Online
http://www.yogajournal.com/

Yoga Life Magazine
http://www.sivananda.org/yogalife/yogalifeindex.htm

AUDIO - MEDITATIONS

Mantell, Susie. Your Present: A Half-Hour of Peace. Relax..Intuit. (914) 769-1122. 1996.

Merrill-Redfield, Sally. The Celestine Meditations: A Guide to Meditating Based on The Celestine Prophecy. Time Warner Audiobooks, 1995.

MUSIC

Anugama- Werner Hagen, Shamanic Dream, Higher Octave Music, 1990.

Anugama- Werner Hagen, Healing, Higher Octave Music, 1990.

Barabas, Tom & Dean Evenston. Soaring, Soundings of the Planet, 1996.

Bernhardt, Patrick. Atlantis Angelis, Atlantis Angelis Network, 1600 de Lorimier, Montreal, Cananda, H2K 3W5.

Coxon, Robert H., The Inner Voyage, R.H.C. Productions & Intermede Communications, 1991.

Enya. The Memory of Trees. Warner Music, 1995.

Enya. Orinoco Flow. Intersound, 1996.

Halpern, Steven. Spectrum Suite. Steven Halpern Sound, 1988.

Halpern, Steven. Zodiac and Starborne Suites. Steven Halpern Sound, 1988.

Hammer, Michael/Yahoel. Heart of the Star. Council of Light, P.O. Box 160, Davenport, CA. (408) 457-2655.

Kater, Peter and R. Carlos Nakai. Honorable Sky. Silver Wave Records, 1994.

Kaur, Singh. Crimson Collection: Vols. 1,2,6,7.

Kenny G, Breathless, Arista Records, 1992.

Kobialka, Daniel. Mind Dance. LiSem Enterprises, Inc., 1984.

Lynch, Ray. Deep Breakfast. Windham Hill Records, 1984.

Osho, Meditations of Osho, Kundalini, Chidvilas, inc., PO Box 17550, Boulder, CO 80308, (303) 449-7811.

Osho, Meditations of Osho, Dynamic, Chidvilas, inc., PO Box 17550, Boulder, CO 80308, (303) 449-7811.

Osho, Meditations of Osho,Chakra Sounds,Chidvilas, Inc., PO Box 17550, Boulder, CO 80308, (303) 449-7811.

Raphael, Music to Disappear In , Hearts of Space Records, P.O. Box 31321, San Francisco, CA 94131

Reiki, Merlin's Magic, Inner Worlds Music, (800) 444-9678.

Relaxation Company, Musical Massage: Vol. 2, 20 Lumber Rd ,Roslyn, NY,11576

Roth, Gabrielle, Bones, Raven Recording, P.O. Box 2034, Red Bank, N.J.07701

Scott, Tony, Music for Zen Meditation, Verve Records, 1965.

Seashore Solitude, Rising Star Records, 710 Lakeview Avenue, Atlanta, Georgia 30308

Shardad, Dream Images. Serenity, 180 W. 25th Street, Upland, CA. (800) 869-1684.

Shrieve, Michael, Transfer Station Blues, Fortuna Records, 1986.

The Best of Silver Wave:Vol 2, The Moon, P.O. Box 7943, Boulder, CO 80306, 1993.

Whitesides - Woo, Rob. Miracles. Serenity, Upland, CA. (800) 869-1684.

Winston, George. December. Windham Hill Records and Music, 1982.

VIDEO

Moyers, Bill. Healing and the Mind; Five Part Series. Ambrose Video Publishing, 1994.

Myss, Caroline. The Energetics of Healing. Two tape series, Ambrose Video Publishing, 1994.

Myss, Caroline. Three Levels of Power and How to Use Them. Sounds True, 1997.

Smith, Kathy. New Yoga. Body Vision, 1994

Yoga Journal's Yoga Series.1: Practice for Relaxation, 2: Practice for Beginners, 3: Practice for Flexibility, 4: Practice for Strength. Healing Arts, 1992.

SOURCES FOR LOCAL MUSIC

Mystic Connection: 1100 South Coast Hwy, Laguna Beach, CA 92651 (949) 494-8781.

Moon Rose: 26711 Verdugo St., San Juan Capistrano, CA 92675 (949) 493-8905.

Final Exam

AIKIDO EXAMINATION QUESTIONS I

1. Briefly explain each of the ten (10) stages of the Zen Bulls and comment on the possible personal value to you of working through each stage.

2. Briefly outline the history of Aikido and compare and contrast the major streams of thought that shaped Aikido.

3. Compare and contrast classical Aikido and modern Aikido.

4. Explain and analyze the concepts of *ki*, *chi*, and *prana*.

5. Write a brief essay analyzing any text from the reading list or from any other source.

AIKIDO EXAMINATION QUESTIONS II

1. Briefly explain the importance of the Basic Movements.

2. Describe a technique and show how it evolved from the Basic Movements.

3. List and briefly explain at least four (4) techniques.

4. Briefly list the benefits of training in Aikido.

5. Write a brief essay analyzing any text from the reading list or from any other source.

AIKIDO EXAMINATION QUESTIONS III

1. Describe in detail and explain the benefits of breakfalls.

2. Describe and explain the functions of techniques.

3. Define and explain the primary function of our training.

4. Describe in detail and explain the *she-te*/*uke* relationship.

5. Write a brief essay analyzing any text from the reading list or from any other source.

YOGA EXAMINATION QUESTIONS I

1. Briefly explain each of the ten (10) stages of the Zen Bulls and comment on the possible personal value to you of working through each stage.

2. Briefly outline the history of Yoga and compare and contrast the major streams of thought that shaped Yoga.

3. Compare and contrast the four (4) types of Yoga.

4. Explain and analyze the concepts of energy fields and the Chakras.

5. Write a brief essay analyzing any text from the reading list or from any other source.

YOGA EXAMINATION QUESTIONS II

1. Briefly explain the eight (8) limbs of Yoga as stated by Patanjali and analyze each stage as it effects "fluctuations of body/mind."

2. Describe the techniques of three (3) Pranayamas and list the benefits of each one.

3. List the benefits and briefly explain at least four (4) techniques of relaxation.

4. Briefly describe and list the benefits of the core program of classic Asanas.

5. Write a brief essay analyzing any text from the reading list or from any other source.

YOGA EXAMINATION QUESTIONS III

1. Describe in detail and explain the benefits of the Sun Salutation.

2. Describe and explain the functions of the Life Centers.

3. Define elemental Yoga and list the appropriate Pranayams and Asanas for each element. (Earth, Water, Fire, Air, Space)

4. Describe in detail and explain the benefits of Buddhaprem's core postures.

5. Write a brief essay analyzing any text from the reading list or from any other source.

ACKNOWLEDGMENTS

Page1,31 From *The Martial Spirit: An Introduction to the Origin and Philosophy and Psychology of the Martial Arts* by Herman Kauz. Copyright © 1988 by Overlook Press. Reprinted with permission.

Page 3 "The Purpose of Martial Art Training" by Daisetz T. Suzuki, From *Zen in the Art of Archery,* Eugen Herrigel, ed. Copyright © 1981,1989 by Random House. Reprinted with permission.

Page 9 "Aikido in the Mind of the West" from *The Ultimate Athlete* by George Leonard. Copyright © 1975 by George Leonard. Reprinted with permission.

Page 19 "The History of Aikido and Its Founder" from *The Forge of the Spirit* by John Donahue. Copyright © 1991 by Garland Publishing. Reprinted with permission.

Page 28 From *Autumn Lightening* by Dave Lowry. Copyright © 1984 by Shambhala Publications, Inc. Reprinted with permission.

Page 41 " A Soft Answer" by Terry Dobson. Originally published in Graduate Review. Reprinted by permission of Werner Erhard and Associates with special permission, December 198, of Readers Digest.

Page 47 From *The Zen Way to the Martial Arts* by Taisen Deshimaru. Copyright © 1982 by Penguin Putnam Inc. Reprinted with permission.

Pages 49,50,57,60,61, 69 From *Zen and Japanese Culture* by Daisetz T. Suzuki Copyright © 1970 by Princeton University Press. Reprinted with permission.

Page 78 "How to Find a Aikido Dojo" by Susan Perry, from *Aikido Today Magazine*. Copyright by Arte Press. Reprinted with pcrmission.

Page 107 "Aikido and Yoga" from *The Secret of Aikido* by John Stevens. Copyright © 1995 by Shambhala Publications, Inc. Reprinted with permission.

Page 121 "The Meaning of Yoga" from *Integral Yoga: A Concept of Harmonious and Creative Living* by Haridas Chaudhuri. Copyright © 1965 by Theosophical Publishing House. Reprinted by permission.

Page 127 "The Four Yogas" by Ganga White. Copyright © 1990 by White Lotus Foundation. Reprinted with permission.

Page 132 From *Some Unrecognized Factors in Medicine* by H. Tudor Edmonds. Copyright © 1976 by Theosophical Publishing House. Reprinted with permission.

Page 217 From Zen Flesh, Zen Bones by Paul Reps. Copyright © 1957 by Paul Reps. Reprinted with permission.